Research in Criminology

Series Editors
Alfred Blumstein
David P. Farrington

Research in Criminology

Understanding and Controlling Crime: Toward A New Research Strategy
David P. Farrington, Lloyd E. Ohlin and James Q. Wilson

The Social Ecology of Crime
J.M. Byrne and R.J. Sampson (Eds.)

The Reasoning Criminal: Rational Choice Perspectives on Offending
Derek B. Cornish and Ronald V. Clarke (Eds.)

The Social Contexts of Criminal Sentencing
Martha A. Myers and Susette M. Talarico

Predicting Recidivism Using Survival Models
Peter Schmidt and Ann Dryden Witte

Coping, Behavior, and Adaptation in Prison Inmates
Edward Zamble and Frank J. Porporino

Prison Crowding: A Psychological Perspective
Paul B. Paulus

Off School, In Court: An Experimental and Psychiatric Investigation of Severe School Attendance Problems
I. Berg, I. Brown and R. Hullin

Policing and Punishing the Drinking Driver: A Study of General and Specific Deterrence
Ross Homel

Judicial Decision Making, Sentencing Policy, and Numerical Guidance
Austin Lovegrove

Criminal Behavior and the Justice System: Psychological Perspectives
Hermann Wegener, Friedrich Lösel and Jochen Haisch (Eds.)

Male Criminal Activity from Childhood Through Youth: Multilevel and Developmental Perspectives
Marc Le Blanc and Marcel Fréchette

continued on page 142

S. Ekland-Olson W.R. Kelly

Justice Under Pressure

A Comparison of Recidivism Patterns Among Four Successive Parolee Cohorts

With 29 Illustrations

With H.-J. Joo, J. Olbrich, and M. Eisenberg

Springer-Verlag
New York Berlin Heidelberg London Paris
Tokyo Hong Kong Barcelona Budapest

Sheldon Ekland-Olson, Ph.D.
Department of Sociology and Dean, University of Texas at Austin, Austin, TX 78712, USA
William R. Kelly, Ph.D.
Department of Sociology, University of Texas at Austin, Austin, TX 78712, USA

Series Editors:

Alfred Blumstein
School of Urban and Public Affairs, Carnegie-Mellon University, Pittsburgh, PA 15213, USA

David P. Farrington
Institute of Criminology, University of Cambridge, Cambridge CB3 9DT, England

Library of Congress Cataloging-in-Publication Data
Ekland-Olson, Sheldon, 1944-
Justice under pressure / Sheldon Ekland-Olson, William R. Kelly.
p. cm.—(Research in criminology)
Includes bibliographical references and index.
ISBN-13:978-1-4613-9519-5
1. Prisons—Texas. 2. Parole—Texas. 3. Criminal justice, Administration of—Texas. 4. Recidivism—Texas. I. Kelly, William R. (William Robert), 1950- . II. Title. III. Series.
HV9475.T4E55 1993
364.9764—dc20 92-42354

Printed on acid-free paper.

Softcover reprint of the hardcover 1st edition 1993

Production coordinated by Chernow Editorial Services, Inc., and managed by Christin R. Ciresi; manufacturing supervised by Jacqui Ashri.
Typeset by Best-set Typesetter Ltd., Hong Kong.

9 8 7 6 5 4 3 2 1

ISBN-13:978-1-4613-9519-5 e-ISBN-13:978-1-4613-9517-1
DOI: 10.1007/978-1-4613-9517-1

Preface

By the late 1980s, it was quite clear that a revolution had taken place in the way the nation's prisons were being built and run. Court-ordered reforms, grounded largely in a concern with overcrowded conditions, brought internal administrative adjustments. These court-induced policy shifts were supplemented and in some cases countered by tough-talking politicians willing to pass a wide range of prison-filling laws. In the process, prison construction became, quite literally, a growth industry.

This was nowhere more apparent than in California, where use-a-gun, go-to-prison laws and other mandatory sanctions were instituted. Almost immediately, media pundits were heard either praising or decrying California's multibillion dollar construction efforts, the first substantial prison construction in the state in twenty years. Those supporting construction challenged not-in-my-backyard protests with consultant reports underscoring the economic benefit prisons offered local economies. These consultant reports, in turn, were countered by you-can't-build-yourself-out-of-the-crime-problem advocates. More money for prisons meant less for job programs and fewer early childhood education and nutrition efforts—i.e., fewer resources to address the very conditions that seemed to be producing the ever-growing supply of criminals.

To many observers, California and other states were embarking on an economic course at once ineffectual and self-destructive. Prisons, which are expensive to build and more expensive to run, were being filled as fast as they were built. There was no detectable letup in the crime rate. Gangs in the state's major metropolitan regions continued to expand. All the while, the nation watched as this massively funded experiment in prison construction unfolded.

It was during the mid-to-late 1980s that Texas began seriously considering a prison construction effort of its own. Prodded by federal court decisions, legislators began contemplating whether to develop alternatives to incarceration or to become players in a catch-up construction game. It was in the climate of this debate that we decided to undertake the research reported in this book.

In their consideration of alternatives to prison, Texas legislators shifted much of the management of the prison population crisis to the Parole Board. The board developed early release strategies as well as scales to predict high-risk parolees. At the same time, the state legislature began laying the groundwork for embarking on a prison-building program, which by the early 1990s would rival the program undertaken in California.

What we wanted to find out was whether this shift in policy made any difference in the crime rate. More particularly, did the shift make any difference in that portion of the crime rate related to the revolving prison door? Were persons released on parole more or less likely to return to prison sooner given the changes taking place in the administration of justice?

To pursue these questions, we approached the research arm of the Board of Pardons and Paroles as well as the Texas Prison System and the Texas Department of Public Safety to secure the relevant data sets. The research would not have been possible without their assistance, and it is hereby gratefully acknowledged. In addition, we applied to the National Institute of Justice and the University Research Institute at the University of Texas at Austin for funding support. These grants, too, were critical to the eventual completion of the project.

The first year and a half we spent collecting, coding, and analyzing the data. Portions of the early findings were reported at professional meetings and eventually published in the *Law and Society Review* (Kelly and Ekland-Olson 1991) and *Crime and Delinquency* (Ekland-Olson, Kelly, and Eisenberg 1992a). Upon publication we became convinced that it was also useful to work on a longer piece that brought all the findings under a single cover. Hence this book.

In preparing this book we have benefitted from the critical efforts of a number of people. Mark Warr, Jim Austin, Tom Pollum, Joan Petersilia, Susan Turner, Pablo Martinez, and Daniel Glaser provided useful comments and assistance on early drafts. Edie Van Cleve was invaluable in the editorial and manuscript preparation phases of the project. Our spouses, Dr. Marie Crane and Carolyn Ekland-Olson, critiqued, prodded, and encouraged our efforts throughout. We are most grateful for their enduring support. Finally, each of the senior authors extends his thanks to the other for his colleagueship in the best sense of that term. The work simply would not have been possible without equal effort throughout.

Ethnicity and the Politics of Editing

Whenever you divide the world into a small number of ethnic categories, say three as we have done in this volume, you seriously distort reality. You gloss over important distinctions. You also run the risk of offending. This point was brought home as we went into the final phases of production. A member of the editorial staff called to inquire, in apologetic tones, about a "sensitive question." It had to do with our use of the term "Anglo." Several colleagues in the editor's office were offended. Why not use the more conventional "White?" The offended were not Anglo they were Greek or Italian, besides wasn't Anglo a derogatory term?

As the conversation continued, the editor related that the only manuscripts she ever saw using Anglo were from the Southwest—Texas, New Mexico, Arizona, and California. She was a bit relieved that Anglo wasn't a derogatory epithet—Gringo was the term she had in mind. Several alternatives were suggested. "White" was problematic since many Hispanics or Latinos considered themselves members of that category. "Americans of European Extraction" might work but it too glossed over differences and was cumbersome. The acronym AMEX might be used, but it carried with it credit card implications and came close to some variation on the often-heard Tex-Mex.

The more we talked the more elusive the resolution became. Was it not also the case that African-American, Hispanic, and Latino glossed over important differences. Many African Americans stop tracing their ancestry in the Caribbean, others in Brazil or other Latin American countries populated by the African diaspora. Among Latinos, Mexican-Americans identify with a different heritage than do persons from Guatemala, El Salvador, Chile, Peru, or Cuba.

In the end, with apologies to our friends in the editor's office and any others who rightly recognize the inaccuracies in any tri-ethnic categorization of ancestral heritage, we decided to stick with our more immediate southwestern surroundings and make comparisons between Latinos, African-Americans, and Anglos.

Contents

1
National Trends and the Assessment of Prison Crowding

In the early 1980s, prison crowding was proclaimed "the most critical administrative problem facing the United States criminal justice system" (Blumstein 1983, 229). While debates emerged over the meaning of "crowding" as the decade unfolded (Sherman and Hawkins 1981; Gaes 1985), there are few today who would dispute that crowded prison conditions were the major driving force for the administration of criminal justice in the 1980s.

By mid-decade, all but eleven states had at least one prison considered "overcrowded," according to the Bureau of Justice Statistics. These conditions were litigated in all but a handful of states. Moreover, the National Institute of Justice reported that the number one problem as perceived by judges, prosecutors, public defenders, and correctional officers was prison crowding. In perception and fact, available cell space along with other measures of the ratio of inmates and resources occupied a central place among criminal justice policymakers. This book is about the pressures generated by these strained resources and in particular how judicial, legislative, and correctional responses to these pressures may have affected crime rates and the prison population.

National Trends—1975 through 1989

Table 1.1 presents annual data on the total number of prisoners incarcerated in state prisons as well as the incarceration rate (i.e., the number of inmates incarcerated per 100,000 resident population). During the fifteen years between 1975 and 1989, the inmate population housed in state facilities grew by 182 percent. In 1975, there were 216,462 inmates in state prisons. By 1985, only ten years later, the prison population had doubled to 436,021. Between 1980 and 1989, the number of state inmates rose by 114 percent. In the last half of the 1980s alone, the number of prisoners increased by 40 percent. Clearly, the decade of the 1980s was one of tremendous growth in the number of persons incarcerated. This

TABLE 1.1. Prisoners in state prisons and the U.S. incarceration rate.

Year	Number of prisoners	Incarceration rate
1975	240,593	111
1976	262,833	120
1977	285,456	129
1978	294,396	132
1979	301,470	133
1980	315,974	138
1981	353,167	153
1982	394,374	170
1983	419,820	179
1984	443,398	188
1985	480,568	200
1986	522,084	216
1987	560,812	228
1988	603,732	244
1989	680,809	271

Source: Bureau of Justice Statistics (1991b).

growth in the prison population far outstripped growth in the general population. During the years between 1975 and 1989, the incarceration rate increased by nearly 150 percent. During the 1980s, the number of inmates per 100,000 population rose by 95 percent, with a substantial increase of 36 percent during the period between 1985 and 1989.[1]

It is important to note that both the absolute size and the rate of growth of the incarcerated population are central to any discussion of policy implications regarding the link between incarceration and the crime rate. As Rosenfeld and Kempf (1991, 486–87) note:

> An adequate assessment of the correctional system in general, and prison crowding in particular, must address not simply the size but also the rate of growth of the population under correctional supervision. Policies designed for a large but stable correctional population may differ considerably from those required by a population that is growing rapidly. Even more striking than the sheer size of the correctional population is its extraordinary growth rate.

[1] Prisoners in federal facilities represent a relatively small proportion of all inmates in prison, averaging between 6 and 8 percent of all inmates during the 1980s. Nevertheless, it is important to note that the federal inmate population has grown relatively rapidly as well. During the period from 1975 to 1989, the federal inmate population rose by 145 percent. The bulk of this growth occurred during the latter half of the 1980s, with the inmate population rising by 103 percent between 1985 and 1989.

The most immediately obvious implication of the large size and rapid expansion of the nation's prison systems is that resources available for paying the high cost of incarceration are going to be sorely strapped. It is estimated that if current trends continue, state prison populations will reach the one million mark by 1994. Assuming more modest growth rates of one-half of the average rate of the late 1980s, it is estimated that the prison population will exceed one million by the year 2000 (Rosenfeld and Kempf 1991).

There is ample evidence that resources to expand the capacity of prison systems have not kept pace with this rapid growth. The Bureau of Justice Statistics (BJS) (1987, 1991a) compiles data comparing the existing prison population with prison capacity. Capacity is determined by examining the rated, operational, and design capacities; then comparisons are made between the inmate population and the highest and lowest reported capacity figures. In 1984, BJS reported that on average, state prisons were operating at 105 percent of their highest capacity and 116 percent of their lowest capacity. By 1990, the average state prison was operating at 115 percent of its highest capacity and 127 percent of its lowest capacity.

It is important to note that the absolute value of these assessments of prison crowding should not be taken at face value. In some states, the rated capacity assumes one inmate per cell. In others, the measure of capacity assumes two inmates per cell. Thus, with the two-person-per-cell definition of prison capacity and assuming all cells were filled to capacity, the prison would be at 100 percent of capacity. With the one-person-per-cell standard, the judgment would be that the prison system was at 200 percent of capacity. While the absolute values are suspect, there is little doubt that levels of crowding have increased.

Whatever the rated capacity, it is most likely the case that as prisons became crowded, inmates began to backup in local jails. With this assumption in hand, another indicator of the trend of increasing prison crowding is the extent to which convicted prisoners who have been sentenced to prison are being housed in local jails. The Bureau of Justice Statistics (1978, 1989b) provides some information on this issue. In 1978, there were an estimated 9,944 prisoners in local jails who should have been transferred to prison facilities. By 1989, that figure had risen to 29,358, representing a 283 percent increase. While the number of prisoners housed in local jails is not large, the trend is indicative of increasing crowding in state facilities.

What accounts for this tremendous growth and the increased levels of crowding? Changes in crime rates constitute one obvious possibility. All else being equal, as crime increases, so should arrests, convictions, and incarcerations. The Uniform Crime Reports, published annually by the Justice Department, provide data on total index crime rates, violent index crime rates, and property index crime rates. What is evident from these data is that the total index crime rates peaked in the early 1980s, declined during the first half of the decade, and then gradually increased from 1984 to 1989. Over the fifteen-year period from 1975 to 1989, total index crimes reported to the police increased by 8.7 percent, a relatively modest gain, reflecting the non-monotonic trend in the crime rate. A somewhat different picture emerges if we focus on the latter half of the decade of the 1980s. Between 1984 and 1989, total index crime rates rose by 14 percent.

There are substantial differences between the trends in violent and property index crime rates. Between 1975 and 1989, violent crime rates increased by 37 percent. The comparable figure for property crimes is 5.8 percent. Once again, however, there were fairly dramatic changes between 1984 and 1989. Violent crime rates rose by 23 percent, and property crime rates rose by 13 percent over this period.

To what extent are changes in index crime rates, as reflected in reports to the police, related to changes in state prison populations? The answer is that there is some correspondence between changes in crime rates and changes in the size of the incarcerated population. For example, the prison population increased by 13.1 percent between 1980 and 1981 and by 12.6 percent between 1981 and 1982, coinciding with the increases in index crimes between 1978 and 1979, and 1979 and 1980. Moreover, the increases in index crimes during the latter half of the 1980s (a 14 percent increase between 1984 and 1989) correspond with increases in the size of the prison population during this same time period (a 51 percent increase). While a comparison of changes in crime rates and the prison population suggests a relationship between the two, it is also clear that this is not the whole story. The magnitude of the increases in crime rates, while consistent with changes in the size of the prison population, are too small to fully account for the rise in the correctional population.

Another factor that likely plays an important role in the size of the inmate population is arrests. All else being equal, as the number of arrests increases, so should the prison population. Data provided by the Bureau of Justice Statistics (1991b) indicate that between 1980 and 1989 arrests for total index crimes increased by 18.9 percent. The comparable figures for violent and property index offenses were 35.3 percent and 14.7 percent respectively. Arrests for aggravated assault and motor vehicle theft had the largest relative growth rates, with percentage increases of 54.6 percent and 49.6 percent respectively.

Looking beyond index offenses, we find that total arrests for all reported offenses increased by 27.7 percent between 1980 and 1989. The one set of offenses in which arrests increased the most over this time period was drug offenses, rising by over 125 percent. Moreover, in 1980, drug offenses constituted 5.7 percent of all reported offenses. By 1989, that had increased to 10 percent.

Thus, it appears that increases in arrests for both index and selected nonindex offenses are consistent with increases in the prison population.

It also appears that drug arrests are particularly important. However, as was the case with increasing crime rates, the increase in arrests accounts for some of the growth in the number of prisoners, but it is not large enough to be responsible for the entire increase in the prison population.

It has also been argued that the prison population has grown because of longer prison sentences and more conservative release policies. In an attempt to address this possibility, Langan (1991, 1572), after compiling state-level data on sentence length and average sentence served, as well as other factors, concluded:

> Prison population growth since 1973 has been driven by increases in prison admissions. To determine the source of growth, various factors that can increase admissions were investigated: changes from 1974 to 1986 in reported crime and arrest rates, in imprisonment rates, in drug arrest and imprisonment rates and in population demographics. Only 9 percent of admission growth from 1974 to 1986 was found to be attributable to changes in reported crime and arrest rates. Changes in drug arrest and imprisonment rates explained only 8 percent. Demographic changes were responsible for a modest amount of growth, explaining 20 percent. By far, the strongest determinant was higher imprisonment rates, explaining 50 percent. As the term was used here, higher imprisonment rates meant more prison sentences for every 100 felony arrests. This occurs when prosecutors obtain more felony convictions or judges give more prison sentences . . . increases in court commitments have been driven not just by more convictions but also by more prison sentences as a percentage of sentences imposed.

Given the rising crime and arrest rates, coupled with an increased tendency to send persons to prison, states have adopted a variety of strategies for dealing with prison crowding, including the "back-door" solution of accelerated parole release. Parole release has been an increasingly popular, quick-fix solution in many states faced with scarce prison space and/or intervention by the federal courts. And as Mullen (1987, 96) argues:

> For the simple reason that most states have centralized control over time served (through parole and other discretionary release mechanisms), it has been far easier to regulate prison populations by adjusting release than by adjusting intake decisions.

There are two basic mechanisms in place for accelerating the parole release of state prison inmates. First, the majority of states have either (1) administrative good time, i.e., good time that serves as credit against time served, or (2) good conduct or meritorious good time, awarded for good behavior or participation in prison programs. Secondly, by 1986, nearly one-third of the states had emergency release legislation in place, providing for the accelerated release of inmates when the prison population reached a predetermined critical level. States with emergency release provisions include Texas, Tennessee, Georgia, Michigan, Illinois, Washington, Iowa, Florida, North Carolina, Virginia, and Colorado, among others.

One important consequence of the increasing reliance on parole release for managing prison populations is the increase in the parole population. In 1980, the total number of inmates on parole from state prisons was slightly under 200,000. In just ten years, the parole population grew by 121 percent, reaching 435,385 in 1989. Changes in the number of parolees per 100,000 resident population (the parole rate) is indicative of the expanded release of inmates from state prisons. In 1980, there were 118 parolees per 100,000 population. By 1989, the rate had risen to 236, representing a 100 percent increase in just ten years.

One obvious question that arises is whether the parole population was growing because time on parole was increasing or because the number of releases was increasing. In fact, both factors come into play. In states which provide for variable time on parole (typically computed as sentence length minus flat time in prison), early releases resulted in somewhat longer time under parole supervision. However, the primary reason for the growth in the parole population was the increase in parole releases. In 1980, state prisons released 113,047 inmates. By 1989, the comparable figure for new parole releases was 294,686, representing a 161 percent increase over that time period.

A Sea-Change in Prisoner Rights

While these broad national trends were unfolding, there was a sea change in the legal rights of prisoners. The debate regarding these rights, and particularly the assessment of prison conditions, was guided by constitutional, statutory, and judicial signposts hammered out in the years immediately following the Civil War. When it came to the conditions of imprisonment, the "slaves of the state" imagery left by these signposts, coupled with a general reluctance of the courts to intervene in the administrative affairs of the state, yielded what would eventually be called the judicial hands-off approach to what went on behind prison walls.

This legal and moral posture toward prison life would not change until the civil rights movement gained momentum following World War II. The initial expansion of rights centered around increased prisoner access to federal courts. This policy of enhanced accessibility provided the foothold for the prisoner rights movement, which eventually reshaped the legitimacy of then-existing conditions of imprisonment (Jacobs 1980). Joining the constitutional protections of freedom of expression, due process, and the prohibition of cruel and unusual punishments with the provisions of the 1871 Civil Rights Act, lawyers and writ-writing inmates secured increased freedoms in the areas of religious rights, protections from severe corporal punishment, and access to lawyers, courts, and legal materials.

Most importantly, in terms of the pressures on prison capacity, federal courts, prodded by activist lawyers, eventually began to examine the totality of conditions within prison walls. It was this final reversal of the hands-off doctrine that led to court-imposed changes based on conclusions regarding the crowded conditions of prison life. By the mid-to-late 1980s the American Civil Liberties Union was able to claim that there were major court orders affecting the quality of life in prisons and jails in forty states. Pressures induced by these prison condition decisions were felt almost immediately throughout the entire criminal justice system from a prisoner's arrest to his or her release on parole.

Assessing the Impact of Litigated Prison Reform

Not surprisingly, court involvement in matters such as prison management policies, early release of prisoners, and state appropriations for improved prison conditions—matters that many consider outside the expertise or jurisdiction of the judiciary—led to a heated debate over the role judges should play in institutional reform and the consequences of judicial intervention.[2] While there has been some attempt to examine the impact of judicial intervention on prison life in the context of the broader social and political arena, most empirical assessments have concentrated on changes within prison walls (Harris and Spiller 1977; Ekland-Olson 1986; Taggart 1989). Feeley and Hanson (1990, pp. 12–46), in an attempt to bring some order to this growing body of literature, have suggested that three sets of issues should be explored: the impact court decisions have had on the structure of correctional institutions; the impact these decisions have had on policies promulgated in the wake of court action; and finally, shifts in the delivery of services within institutions that have been brought about through court intervention.

Structural reform studies are defined by research into the shifts in patterns of authority, safety, and violence within prison walls, as well as investigations of changes in institutional morale and leadership, and modernization of the correctional bureaucracy. This has included such practices as sleeping arrangements, availability of medical care, and the conduct of disciplinary hearings, as well as the effects of broader changes

[2] It was a debate that went beyond the issues of prison reform to address court intervention in educational and mental health institutions as well. See, for example, Abram Chayes, "The Role of the Judge in Public Law Litigation," 89 *Harvard Law Review* 1281 (1976); Donald L. Horowitz, *The Courts and Social Policy*, Washington, D.C.: Brookings Institution, 1977; Paul Mishkin "Federal Courts as State Reformers," 35 *Washington and Lee Law Review*, 949 (1978); John Hart Ely, *Democracy and Distrust*, Cambridge: Harvard University Press, 1980.

in state budgets, and the federal government's attempt to reform prison accreditation standards. Finally, when all is said and done, Feeley and Hansen note that one essential purpose of court intervention has been to improve the nature and quality of services provided to inmates. Thus, assessments of court-induced changes should include the effectiveness and quality of service delivery as measured by such outcomes as access to medical care, privacy, exercise, food, and legal assistance.

The research reported in the following chapters, while related to these dimensions of assessment, proceeds from a somewhat different set of premises. In addition to the structural, policy, and service-delivery changes fashioned from court decisions, it is important to know in a broader systemic sense if there has been any impact on the criminal justice system from court-induced changes in the way prisons are run. Given these systemic changes, it is also important to determine what impact they in turn may have had on crime rates.

It is undeniable that responses to crowded prison conditions have been systemic in their implications. Police know the prisons and jails are full and adjust their arresting practices and more discretionary actions accordingly. Judges expand their use of probation in large measure because bulging prison and jail facilities dictate that they do so. Prison officials, charged with managing inmate flow through prisons—the so-called revolving-door syndrome—have likewise shifted thresholds for good-time credits and thus parole eligibility to free up bed space. Finally, and to bring the system full circle through such mechanisms as "technical revocations," parole officers have adjusted their decisions to accommodate the increasingly stressed mix of resources in the criminal justice system. It has become routine among those debating the responses to the systemic strains induced by crowded prisons to categorize such responses into front-door, capacity management, and back-door remedies.

Given the strain on existing facilities, pilot programs have experimented with such alternatives as intensive supervision caseloads, shock incarceration or prison "boot camps," and electronic monitoring for home incarceration. Assessments of these alternatives to incarceration have begun to appear in the literature. The evidence is still too sparse to reach firm conclusions, but findings have not always been encouraging. For example, in a study comparing probation and incarceration in California in 1985, Petersilia and Turner stated, "The majority of felons who are placed on probation in California constitute a serious threat to the public and the increasing use of probation as a sentence for felons is a high-risk gamble" (1986, v). These researchers also concluded, however, that current high-cost incarceration practices fared little better. On balance they note:

> the U.S. criminal justice system might be able to get additional return on the resources that are actually or potentially available by examining the benefits

and costs of various intermediate-level sanctions for felony offenders, such as community-based programs that provide more intensive supervision than routine probation but are less restrictive (and less expensive) than prison. (1986, xi)

These intensive supervision programs (ISPs) have been implemented across the country with the stated purpose of reducing prison populations in ways that do not trivialize the offense or unacceptably increase the risk to the public. Early efforts in the 1970s, which tended to be rehabilitative in emphasis, were not encouraging (see an early review in Banks et al. [1977]). More recent ISPs, designed to reduce pressures on crowded prisons, have shifted their focus more toward surveillance and control. Again, reviews of these relatively new programs reveal results not in line with what the program designers might have hoped for (e.g., Byrne, Lurigio, and Baird 1989). In a follow-up study to their comparative analysis of probation and incarceration in California, Petersilia and Turner reviewed the intensive supervision programs begun in Georgia, New Jersey, Illinois, and New York in preparation for yet another effort in Oregon. From this review they reached three conclusions (1986, 3):

- While the primary stated goal of most ISP programs is to relieve prison crowding, very few true prison-diversion ISP programs have been implemented.
- Even where such programs do exist, procedures are such that one is unsure whether truly prison-bound offenders are participating.
- In the programs where procedures are in place to assure that only prisoners participate, no true experimental comparisons using random assignment are being conducted, thus prohibiting a credible assessment of the program's effects on costs and public safety.

A major portion of the disappointing performance of ISPs as an alternative to prison can be traced to the fact that instead of diverting persons from prison, ISPs have been used to increase the severity of probation conditions. Thus, this alternative to incarceration, like other related alternatives such as prison boot camps and efforts at electronic monitoring, has resulted in a net-widening effect wherein more convicted felons are brought under increased supervision, but not with the result of reducing the pressures on prison resources (McKenzie and Parent 1991).

Lamenting this net-widening tendency, Morris and Tonry (1990, 9) have argued that the efforts at developing alternatives to incarceration have been defective in both theory and practice:

In theory, it is an error to see intermediate punishments as any more an alternative to imprisonment than an alternative to ordinary probation. In practice, it has not been shown that intermediate punishments much reduce the pressure on scarce cell space because they draw their subjects at least as much from those who would not have been incarcerated as from those who would.

As a result, the hope that front-door alternatives to incarceration would relieve pressures on crowded prisons and thereby save the taxpayers money has not been realized. Rather than abandon the promise held out by a wider range of punishments, Morris and Tonry (1990, 10) argue for what they call a more "principled" sentencing system. A principled sentencing system

> . . . differs from the usual in-or-out and, if in, for-how-long system. It substitutes principles that allow for interchangeability between imprisonment and intermediate punishments and for interchangeability between probation and intermediate punishments. . . . Below a level of severity of crime punishable by, say, 2 years' imprisonment, crime prevention purposes and a humane economy of punishment require principled interchangeability between punishments to be served in prison and punishments to be served in the community and also between probation and more severe or restrictive community-based punishments.

Such principled interchangeability of punishments has yet to be refined, and thus the use of front-door alternatives to incarceration continues to be driven by the political climate of particular communities and the organizational demands of crowded prisons and jails. To more directly deal with the crowded condition of jails and prisons, building programs have been initiated across the country. These building programs—along with other strategies such as policies regulating the awarding of good-time credits for time served and mechanisms for emergency releases when prison capacity is overwhelmed—are collectively referred to as capacity-management strategies.

In an analysis of the link between judicial action and state spending on corrections in the first ten states subject to federal court intervention, Taggart (1989), looking at all ten states collectively, concluded that the effect of court intervention was small, but that what link there was came in increases on the capital side of the budget, "Undoubtedly . . . in the form of new prison construction." In a reanalysis of Taggart's data, Feeley rightly notes that this overall assessment hides quite dramatic regional variation. Federal court intervention had its greatest budgetary impact on prisons in the South where court decisions "altered the vision and often the guiding principles of corrections officials and have helped reshape the structure and organization of jails and prisons" (1989, 280).

While the impact of federal court intervention may have been most evident in the South, by far the most ambitious prison construction program was launched in California in the 1980s. By the end of the decade the Blue Ribbon Commission on Inmate Population Management issued its assessment of this effort (1990). Over the decade the number of persons confined in California's prisons had almost quadrupled from 23,000 to 87,000. Given estimated per-cell construction costs ranging from $16,000 to $50,000, depending on the level of security and the type of construction involved, along with the per-inmate operating costs of from $13,000 to $20,000, depending again on the level of security and type of services required, this quadrupling of the prison capacity became a budgetary sinkhole and an alternative that few states were able or willing to undertake.

Instead, a number of alternative capacity-management strategies were employed. Michigan provides an example, repeated with variation in states across the country. In 1979 Michigan voters, angered by the perceived threat of crime and the image that convicted felons were not serving their full sentences, repealed a prison good-time law through referendum (Proposal B). This repeal produced an almost immediate increase in prison population pressures and a decreased ability of prison officials to deal with the accompanying problems. In 1980 Proposal E, a proposal to expand the capacity of Michigan's prison system, was rejected by these same voters. In the face of increased demands and reduced powers, prison staff morale fell, labor-management disputes arose within the prison walls, and the control of the inmate population suffered.

In May of 1981, inmate riots occurred in a number of Michigan prisons. The governor set up the Special Committee on Prison Disturbances to investigate the situation and on August 4, 1981 received the committee's report (1981) that concluded:

> [The passage of Proposal B], coupled with the public's demand that governmental spending be curtailed, tougher laws be passed and longer sentences be imposed, has the net effect of sending more people to prison for longer periods of time without the Department of Corrections being given the resources to meet the extra load. . . . The resulting overcrowding has the devastating effect on prison programs and prison operation. . . . Prison officials are then left with the enormous responsibility of maintaining order under increasingly difficult circumstances.

In response to the bind created by voter preference for increased penalties and voter reluctance to spend more money, Michigan gave the governor "emergency powers" to deal with crowded prison conditions with selective early releases. This basic scenario would be repeated in a number of states across the country, including Texas. In the end, this series of events meant that the management of prison capacity increasingly shifted to the shoulders of those waiting at the back door of the prison—parole boards and officers.

Even in California, where prison construction proceeded at an unprecedented pace, the parole officials found themselves confronting ever-increasing demands. Evidence began to accumulate that the growing paroled population was coming back to prison at increased rates, and one study claimed that the proportion of paroled inmates returning to prison had almost doubled in the early years of the 1980s (Austin 1987). The irony was obvious. The desire to get tougher on crime, coupled with the hesitancy to generate necessary tax revenues, meant that the revolving door of arrest, conviction, sentencing, release, rearrest, reconviction, etc., was spinning with increased speed. It is the purpose of the following chapters to investigate this process, which occurred in virtually every populous state in the Union, by looking closely at a single case study. The primary focus is on an assessment of the short- and longer-term consequences of the strategies implemented for managing prison crowding in Texas.

Chapter 2 examines in detail how the crime rate, prison sentencing, shifting judicial standards, public pressures, and legislative actions set the stage for "the crime problem" between the mid-1970s and the end of the 1980s in Texas. Chapters 3 through 6 present an in-depth look at data collected to address the question of whether these forces resulted in any change in the probability and pattern in which persons returned to prison, with special attention to variation across four cohorts of parolees as well as to a cohort released under emergency provisions during critical crowding periods. Chapter 7 is an assessment of the link between incarceration and crime with a comparison of responses to the crime problem during the 1980s in Texas and California, two states that took very different approaches to addressing the pressures generated by increased levels of prison crowding. Finally, we discuss the major findings and policy implications of this research in chapter 8.

2
Population, Political, and Judicial Pressures on the Texas Criminal Justice System

The Texas Prison Crowding Crisis

In the early 1970s, the Texas prison population fluctuated between 16,000 and 18,000 inmates. By 1981, it had risen to over 30,000, and by 1990, even with stringent population caps in place, it was just under 50,000 (table 2.1).

Increased admissions, as opposed to longer sentences, were the primary source of the burgeoning prison population. Between 1972 and 1981, admissions doubled—from 7,725 to 15,702. During the period 1981 to 1990, they more than tripled again—from 15,702 to 46,290. The organizational impact of this increase on the stability of the Texas Department of Corrections (TDC) prisoner population was dramatic. The ratio of inmates received to total population was roughly fifty-fifty in the early 1970s. It had risen to 94 percent by 1990 (table 2.1).

What produced this rapid growth in admissions? Increasing crime was one factor. During the 1970s and 1980s, the Texas crime index rose by approximately 175 percent. The greatest increase was in property crime (188 percent), but increases in reported violent offenses were also significant (82 percent). Predictably, arrests also increased. The number of arrests for violent offenses rose by some 45 percent, while property offense arrests rose by just over 70 percent.

In addition to the pressure of increased crime and subsequent arrests, some argued that courts were more likely to convict and send persons to prison in a general crackdown on crime. However, when relevant data are examined, the ratio of arrests to convictions has remained quite stable in recent years in Texas. Thus, change in the probability of conviction, given an arrest, has not appreciably affected the dramatic increase in prison admissions during the 1970s and 1980s. On the other hand, courts have increasingly sentenced convicted offenders to prison during the last decade.

Between 1976 and 1987 the ratio of convictions to prison sentences rose by 35 percent, from .23 to .31 (table 2.2). Thereafter they began to

TABLE 2.1. Total on-hand prison population and the ratio of total received to total on-hand population.

Year	Total on-hand population	No. received	Ratio
1972	16,171	7,725	.48
1973	16,689	7,780	.47
1974	16,956	8,217	.49
1975	18,151	9,358	.52
1976	20,976	10,554	.50
1977	20,862	11,077	.53
1978	24,615	12,894	.52
1979	25,164	13,041	.52
1980	28,543	14,176	.50
1981	30,315	15,702	.52
1982	34,393	18,837	.55
1983	36,769	22,870	.62
1984	35,772	23,058	.64
1985	37,320	25,365	.68
1986	38,246	30,471	.80
1987	39,652	35,007	.88
1988	39,664	33,816	.85
1989	41,626	33,303	.80
1990	49,157	46,290	.94

Source: Texas Department of Corrections (1972–1990).

TABLE 2.2. Total criminal court convictions, total new receives to texas department of corrections, and the ratio of total new receives to total convictions.

Year	Total convictions	Total receives	Ratio
1970	28,701	5,853	.20
1971	33,466	6,928	.21
1972	35,244	7,117	.20
1973	36,698	7,140	.19
1974	37,693	7,442	.20
1975	43,762	8,533	.19
1976	42,524	9,626	.23
1977	44,303	9,910	.22
1978	49,702	11,201	.23
1979	52,412	11,432	.22
1980	49,684	12,126	.24
1981	49,092	13,455	.27
1982	58,757	15,539	.26
1983	63,730	17,981	.28
1984	59,801	16,773	.28
1985	59,793	17,534	.29
1986	66,668	20,798	.31
1987	75,204	23,457	.31
1988	74,582	21,218	.28
1989	84,587	19,924	.23

Source: Texas Department of Corrections (1970–1989).

TABLE 2.3. Percent of admissions with no prior confinements.

Year	% No prior confinement	
	TDC	Other prisons
1976	76.1	90.6
1977	76.4	90.1
1978	75.4	90.1
1979	77.3	90.7
1980	78.3	90.5
1981	78.9	89.9
1982	80.5	90.1
1983	82.8	91.1
1984	82.6	90.9
1985	83.3	92.3
1986	85.1	92.5
1987	85.7	94.1
1988	85.4	94.2
1989	84.8	94.5
1990	82.6	95.3

Source: Texas Department of Corrections (1976–1990)

decline as the likelihood of being sent to prison increased, the composition of those sent to TDC shifted. According to TDC admission records, between 1976 and 1990 the percentage of persons admitted with no prior record of confinement in TDC ("first timers") increased from 76 percent to 83 percent of the incoming inmates (table 2.3).

In this sense, persons arriving at TDC came with increasingly less-serious prior records between the mid-1970s and the late 1980s. An increasing proportion of these newly convicted felons were sent to prison for drug trafficking offenses, an increase from 9 percent to 26 percent between 1980 and 1990. At the same time, persons convicted of the two most serious violent offenses—homicide and robbery—constituted a decreasing proportion of yearly admissions—from 21 percent in 1980 to 12 percent in 1990 (table 2.4).

Pressure from the Media

The irony is obvious. The crackdown on crime meant that new pressures on prison capacity came from less-violent offenders. The major release valve in Texas as well as in many other states for this pressure was parole. Between 1980 and 1990, parole and mandatory supervision releases increased by 420 percent from 7,100 to 37,000 (table 2.5).

At times, the system of criminal justice seemed to be standing on its head. As first-time offenders were coming in the front door, highly publicized violent offenders were being let out the back. One of the more

TABLE 2.4. Proportion of total admission to Texas Department of Corrections by offense category.

Year	Homicide and robbery	Burglary	Drugs
1977	21.1	31.5	12.5
1978	21.5	30.2	10.9
1979	22.6	29.3	10.4
1980	20.6	30.0	8.9
1981	20.3	30.5	8.8
1982	20.0	29.8	8.9
1983	18.6	29.0	9.8
1984	16.9	28.1	11.8
1985	15.5	30.3	11.7
1986	14.5	30.0	14.1
1987	13.5	29.0	16.8
1988	12.8	28.6	19.0
1989	12.9	28.5	22.0
1990	12.4	26.8	26.0

Source: Texas Department of Corrections (1977–1990).

infamous instances involved the "Choker" rapist who was convicted and sentenced to 123 years in 1977 for three aggravated rapes and two burglary charges. After serving fewer than eight years in prison, he was released on parole. Shortly thereafter, he was reconvicted for aggravated sexual assault and resentenced to prison.

Over the ensuing months papers across Texas ran articles featuring numerous similar cases, the most dramatic of which involved an inmate who, along with two other inmates, stabbed a fourth inmate to death. A year after the fatal stabbing, this inmate, with a documented lengthy record of violence both inside and outside prison, was released on parole. A few months after release, he was arrested for the rape, robbery, and sodomizing of two women at knife point. Once convicted, his new sentence was thirty years in prison. The media reported he was immediately placed in a trusty status that allowed him special privileges and the possibility of early release. While the stories in the media were not totally accurate and focused on the sensational, the message was clear. Justice in Texas was terribly flawed.

While clear in the media, the image of parole generated from such highly publicized cases was only partially accurate. The prison system was operating under increased pressure. Persons were being released after serving an ever-smaller fraction of their sentences (table 2.6). At the same time, there was an expanding core of inmates in the TDC who were sentenced under the Texas' aggravated offender statute. At the end of fiscal year 1983 there were 6,781 such convicted felons, or 19 percent of the inmate population. By the end of fiscal year 1988, this number had grown to 12,102, or 31 percent of the population. In this sense, prison

TABLE 2.5. TDC inmates discharged, released on parole, released on mandatory supervision, and shock probation.

Year	Discharged	Paroled	Mandatory supervision	Shock probation	Total released
1972	3,420	3,184	0	0	6,604
1973	3,245	3,749	0	0	6,994
1974	3,680	4,138	0	0	7,819
1975	3,037	4,958	0	0	7,995
1976	3,417	4,208	0	0	7,625
1977	3,550	7,477	0	0	11,027
1978	3,647	5,076	10	0	8,733
1979	3,040	7,800	762	0	11,602
1980	2,430	5,072	2,108	*	9,610
1981	1,928	7,465	3,331	*	12,724
1982	1,473	7,453	4,538	*	13,464
1983	1,997	8,588	7,715	1,846	20,146
1984	1,719	9,989	10,055	1,723	23,486
1985	416	9,328	11,864	1,725	23,333
1986	316	14,428	12,751	1,852	29,347
1987	229	19,900	11,681	1,560	33,370
1988	146	24,654	7,631	997	33,428
1989	125	24,673	5,429	676	30,903
1990	120	33,181	3,856	884	38,041

Source: Texas Department of Corrections (1972–1990).
* Shock Probation Figures were not available for 1980, 1981, and 1982

TABLE 2.6. Sentences and time served for persons released from TDC.

Fiscal year	Average years sentenced	Average length of stay	Percent of sentence served
1977	7.56	2.50	33
1978	6.56	2.38	36
1979	6.93	2.42	35
1980	6.45	2.39	37
1981	6.49	2.36	36
1982	6.64	2.35	35
1983	7.96	2.27	28
1984	9.45	2.37	25
1985	8.02	2.02	25
1986	7.73	1.96	25
1987	7.38	1.64	22
1988	7.72	1.74	22
1989	8.20	1.70	21
1990	9.40	1.90	20

Source: Texas Department of Corrections (1977–1990).

beds were being used increasingly for persons convicted of more serious charges.

The composite picture of criminal justice was thus mixed, with two parts to the story. There was a rotating stream of prisoners seemingly walking through the prison's revolving doors. At the same time, the prison's stable population was "hardening," i.e., increasingly composed of more serious offenders. At the foundation of both the revolving door and the hardening prison population was *Ruiz v. Estelle*.

Pressure from the Federal Court

In *Ruiz*, the entire prison system had been declared unconstitutional as of 1981. The primary reason was prison crowding. TDC prisons, Judge William Wayne Justice concluded, were "strained beyond their limitations, currently housing over 200 percent of their original design capacity." This crowding, the judge further stated, exercised a "malignant effect on all aspects of inmate life." It was not just a matter of available space. Services were strained beyond the breaking point. Security was suspect. Inmates were being used to control other inmates. Medical care "persistently and predictably" failed to meet the legitimate needs of the inmate population. An overworked, underfunded staff relied on arbitrary and capricious discipline. Programs for mentally retarded inmates were totally inadequate. The judge's list went on and on.

In 1981, population projections signaled that things were likely to get worse in the 1980s, as indeed they did. Construction plans for large maximum security facilities could not, in the judge's mind, keep pace with the soaring commitment rates. In the court's opinion, TDC should develop less costly, more rapidly expandable alternatives to maximum security incarceration such as honor farms or work camps, halfway houses, and urban work-release centers. Prison officials were to reduce the prisoner population by reviewing good-time awards and parole eligibility factors as well as by expanding work furlough programs, similar in many ways to the program George Bush's campaign would eventually use against Michael Dukakis in the presidential election of 1988.

Such alternatives would, in the court's opinion, relieve overcrowded conditions and save the taxpayers money. They would also come up against a widespread lock-'em-up-and-throw-away-the-key philosophy. With Judge Justice's decree, issued on April 20, 1981, the battle lines over the future of criminal justice in Texas were drawn.

By November 1, 1981, the number of persons incarcerated in the TDC was to be reduced to a number "equal to twice the number of general population cells, plus the number of prisoners who (could) be housed in dormitories at forty square feet per prisoner." After November 1, 1981, the prison system was prohibited from receiving prisoners beyond this defined capacity. Continued progress was mandated for 1982 and by November 1, 1983, all prisoners in the TDC were to be housed in single cells.

This pressure was felt during the Sixty-seventh Session of the Texas legislature in the spring of 1981. A number of bills were passed, including funds to expand the use of parole. There was also an awareness that the court's ruling, if followed to the letter, would cost the state billions of dollars over the next several years. Lawyers for the state decided to appeal.

While the appeal of the *Ruiz* ruling was running its course, the prison population continued to expand. By 1982, it rose to just over 34,000. A crisis point was reached on May 10, 1982. On this date, TDC officials announced a freeze on accepting any more prisoners to avoid violation of the population caps set by Judge Justice. In a brief statement, the Texas Board of Corrections announced its decision.

> The Texas Board of Corrections received a report this morning that shows the prison system is out of compliance with the square footage requirement of the court's order. This is in spite of all the efforts of speeding construction and emergency housing. The prison population projections were wrong mainly because more prisoners have been sent to prison by the courts and fewer prisoners have been paroled than projected by the Board of Pardons and Paroles.
>
> Therefore, the Texas Board of Corrections, after considering all reasonable alternatives, hereby instructs the Director and his staff to accept no further inmates until the prison system can maintain compliance. The Director was also instructed to devise a plan to resume receiving prisoners in a manner to maintain compliance with the Court Order. Resumption of reduced admissions is anticipated within thirty days.

Such announcements are the stuff of which interagency conflicts are made. Within twenty-four hours, Harris County officials in Houston decided to send eighty-two prisoners to TDC regardless of the freeze. These prisoners were refused admission. The next day the prison system's director, W. J. Estelle, received notice to appear before a state judge in Houston to show cause why he should not be held in contempt for refusing to admit the prisoners. Judge Justice responded with a temporary restraining order on the state's contempt hearings. A direct conflict between the federal and state courts was avoided by the immediate release of 450 inmates on parole, followed over the next two months by the accelerated release of another 1,200 parolees. While useful as a temporary measure, this emergency release did not solve the underlying problem. Eventually, several counties would join forces in a suit against the state for not accepting convicted felons—a suit which remained active until the 1980s drew to a close. The freeze, subsequent emergency release, and resulting interagency tension did, however, generate immediate legislative action.

The Legislative Response

In a special session during the last week in May 1982, the legislature appropriated $58 million for prison construction and increased staffing demands. In addition, the governor set up a commission to develop a master plan "to carry the state's correction system into the twenty-first century." While the master plan was never published, recommendations of this committee prompted passage of a series of laws in 1983 aimed at managing the prison system's population.

As the governor's commission was developing its recommendations, appeal proceedings in *Ruiz* were in their final stages. The circuit court affirmed Judge Justice's factual findings but narrowed his remedies for crowding. Most importantly, in a wait-and-see posture, the circuit court vacated Judge Justice's single-celling-by-1983 demand, noting its $300 million price tag. It was better, the circuit court judges felt, to give the state latitude to develop less-costly measures first. If these did not work, additional measures could be mandated.

When the Texas legislature met in 1983, the prison population was approaching 37,000. Faced with this continued expansion and pressure from the courts, the legislature enacted more liberal good-time allowances as well as the Prison Management Act (PMA), which shifted major responsibility for managing the prisoner population to the Board of Pardons and Paroles.

The most important provision of the PMA was its 95 percent of capacity standard, patterned after a Michigan statute, which itself had been prompted by that state's own prison crisis. Given the statutorily defined capacity standard, the PMA mandated that when the prison system's population reached 94 percent of the defined capacity, the governor was to be notified and weekly written reports were to be filed until the population was reduced, in part through the liberalized administrative good-conduct time statute.

If the prison population reached 95 percent or more of the defined capacity, the governor was to be notified in writing and thirty days of "administrative good time" awarded to inmates in specified security and offense categories. Within thirty days of this notice, the governor would certify that an emergency overcrowding situation did indeed exist. Once certified, parole eligibility was to be advanced, in thirty-day increments, to a total of ninety days, or until the prison population was reduced below the 95 percent of capacity cut-off point.

The impact of these legislative measures was immediate and dramatic. Total yearly releases from the TDC rose from just over 13,000 in 1982 to just over 20,000 in 1983, a 50 percent increase in just one year. In 1990, 38,041 inmates were released (table 2.5). These 38,041 parolees constituted seventy-five percent of the total prison population, in 1990! Between 1982 and 1990 the average length of stay in prison for released

TABLE 2.7. Average yearly cost per inmate in texas.

Fiscal year	Average inmate cost-per-year
1977	$2,670.55
1978	2,610.59
1979	2,679.41
1980	3,152.43
1981	3,577.08
1982	4,421.48
1983	5,318.13
1984	6,477.15
1985	7,663.06
1986	9,150.21
1987	9,833.74
1988	11,920.45
1989	12,436.00
1990	13,516.00

Source: Texas Department of Corrections (1977–1990).
The calculation of costs was based on cash expenditures for maintenance of inmates. The calculation excludes other expenses of the state such as some construction projects, Windham School System operation, University of Texas Medical Branch expenses for treating TDC inmates, and employee fringe benefits.

inmates dropped from 2.3 to 1.9 years, and the percentage of sentence served dropped from 35 percent to 20 percent (table 2.6). The percent of sentence served has dropped even further, to 13 percent in 1992.

In 1984, for the first time since the early 1970s, the average monthly inmate population actually declined. While it began to increase again in 1985, the PMA clearly had the desired effect in that by 1987 the number of persons incarcerated in the TDC had leveled off at just over 39,000 inmates. This was welcome news for a state recovering from a severe economic downturn and thus low on resources for such expensive items as the construction of maximum security prisons.

In addition to construction costs, the estimated operating costs associated with housing inmates was skyrocketing. In 1979, the year the *Ruiz* case went to trial, the estimated yearly operating cost per inmate was about $2,700. By 1984, this had risen to an estimated $6,500. In fiscal year 1989, the yearly cost per inmate was estimated to be somewhere between $12,000 and $14,000, depending on costs included in the calculation (table 2.7). At the same time, when the legislature convened in 1987, the state was threatened with fines of up to $800,500 per day for failure to comply with *Ruiz*-mandated reforms.

With the possibility of these fines staring him in the face, Governor-elect William Clements set up a meeting with Judge Justice before taking office in 1987 to discuss the *Ruiz* litigation. Shortly after this meeting,

Clements was quoted in the press as saying, "Let me state quite clearly the facts of the contempt citation handed down by Judge Justice prior to my taking office: We must get in compliance as quickly as possible. We have no choice" (Martin and Ekland-Olson 1987, 245).

The first order of business of the Seventieth Legislature was passage of a $12.6 million emergency appropriation to bring TDC into compliance with the issues raised in the contempt proceedings. Before adjournment, the state's senators and representatives approved some $500 million in general obligation bonds for prison expansion and maintenance. By 1990, many new prison beds had become available and the prison population rose to just under 50,000, for an estimated yearly operating cost of $664.4 million.

In the context of these economic pressures, alternatives to existing practices became evermore attractive. One alternative was to look to the private sector. After some debate over the pitfalls of coupling profit with civil rights as well as the pros and cons of turning the state's criminal justice system into a privately operated growth industry, the 1987 legislature included funds for four privately run five-hundred–bed prerelease centers as part of a broader plan to expand the prison system's capacity. The first of these facilities for minimum- and medium-security inmates opened its doors in Kyle, Texas, in June 1989 amid promises that it would not only save the state money over the years of its operation but also provide a much-needed economic stimulus to the local economy. It would remain for the Seventy-first Legislature in 1989 to enact legislation for sweeping reforms and restructuring of the entire criminal justice system in Texas.

Pressure Moves to the Parole System

As population pressures on the prison system came under control, albeit expensive control, the state's parole system began shouldering a dramatically increased burden. In the mid-1970s, the number of persons released on parole hovered between 4,000 and 5,000. By 1990, after a steady upward trend, the number of persons released in that year under some form of supervision peaked at just over 37,000.

One important consequence of rising parole releases was the increase in the relative size of the parole population compared to the total adult population (table 2.8). In every year, Texas ranked second to Washington, D.C. in terms of the relative size of the parole population. Even more telling is the comparison of the relative increase in the Texas rate and the national rate over this five-year period. Between 1983 and 1989, the national parole rate increased by 84 percent, to 248 per 100,000 population. The rate for Texas increased by 189 percent, to 758 per 100,000 adults.

TABLE 2.8. Number of parolees per 100,000 adult population.

Year	U.S.	Texas
1983	135	290
1984	155	362
1985	158	410
1986	184	489
1987	201	570
1988	213	657
1989	248	758
1990	—	903

Source: Bureau of Justice Statistics (1991b).

All of this, of course, meant a huge increase in the number of parole decisions that had to be made by the Board of Pardons and Paroles and an equally large increase in parole officer caseloads. In 1982, the average parole officer caseload was 67 parolees. By 1986, this had peaked at 93 (table 2.9).

Under these less than ideal conditions, it is not at all surprising that "mistakes" in parole decisions were made. Clearly changes were called for. Prior to the legislative reforms of 1983, there were three members on the Board of Pardons and Paroles as well as the governor, who had the authority to veto the Board's decisions. In 1983, legislation was passed and subsequently approved by the voters of Texas to double the size of the Board and to remove the Governor's veto power.

To further streamline the process and to help Board members reach more consistent and informed decisions as they attempted to review an

TABLE 2.9. Offenders under parole supervision in Texas.

Year	Number of offenders under parole supervision	Supervision caseload per officer
1980	11,933	—
1981	15,466	—
1982	19,584	67:1
1983	24,372	71:1
1984	31,462	81:1
1985	34,813	92:1
1986	41,697	93:1
1987	46,821	90:1
1988	52,047	74:1
1989	62,624	72:1
1990	72,693	84:1

Source: Texas Board of Pardons and Paroles (1980–1989).

ever-increasing number of cases, a numerical rating system was adopted in September 1983. Patterned after scoring systems used in other states and in the federal system, it was hoped that this more-objective standard would take some of the guesswork out of parole decisions. The scale gave potential parolees varying points for personal characteristics and prior criminal record. For example, an inmate coming up for parole would get three points if there was no prior conviction and zero points if there were three or more prior felony convictions. If the victim was injured in the crime of record, the individual would receive no points, if no injury was recorded, one point was scored. In total, some twenty factors were included (appendix A).

When first implemented in September 1983, the scale was hailed as a major step forward. The executive director of the Parole Board suggested that the scale was "like a ray of sunlight," a statistical model that would allow the Parole Board to maintain quality. In practice, the bright promise dimmed. The scale was designed to increase paroles and thereby control the prison population, but on a statistical basis that would minimize the danger to the public. A little over a year after its implementation, evaluation studies suggested it was doing neither. The major reason was straightforward. As more and more inmates were released, the pool of eligible persons became more hard-core. In a sampling of 1981 parole-eligible inmates, an estimated 20 percent were classified as high-risk. According to Board of Pardons and Paroles records, by 1984, high-risk inmates constituted approximately 33 percent of the parole-eligible pool. This meant that there was increased pressure to release persons scoring in the high-risk category. Thus, the Parole Board found itself doubly accused for not acting fast enough to reduce prison crowding and at the same time for making riskier releases. While the prison population did in fact decrease in 1984, by mid-1985 the headcount was consistently hovering around 95 percent of the legislatively defined capacity and thus close to keying the emergency release provisions of the PMA. In response, the Board of Pardons and Paroles began releasing proportionately more parole-eligible inmates.

At first, the door was opened for brief intervals. For several months the Parole Board would approve 35 to 40 percent of the potential parolees. Then approvals would jump to 50 percent, only to fall back to the 35 percent range in the next month. However, by early 1986 the total parole release rate was stabilizing near the 60 percent mark, and more importantly the approval of parole after the first review was leveling off to between 60 and 70 percent of initial-hearings. By 1988, the release-at-initial-hearing rate was fluctuating between 70 to 80 percent (Kelly and Ekland-Olson 1992).

Even with these liberal release measures, the Parole Board did not keep pace with prison population pressures. Parole officials found themselves in a double bind. On the one hand, they were being pressured to manage the crowding crisis in the Texas prison system. This meant that prison beds and parole revocations had to be treated like precious resources. On the other hand, there was what came to be known as the "Willie Horton factor" in the national presidential campaign of 1987 and 1988. In Texas, as elsewhere, there was increased media attention and consequent political pressure and public concern over the release of dangerous felons and, more generally, over the revolving prison door. In Texas, instead of the weekend furlough of Willie Horton, newspapers carried stories about the early release of the "Choker Rapist" and the "Animal."

Media and political pressure surrounding the release of convicted felons reached a peak in 1986 and 1987. It was also during this basic time frame that the total number of persons released from TDC increased approximately 43 percent (from 23,300 to 33,300), an unusually large increase, even in this time of transition. This increased volume meant that the Parole Board was confronted with an increasingly high-risk pool of parole candidates. To compensate, parole officers could respond to the heightened public concern through increased use of technical revocations when there were indications that parolees were getting into trouble or committing new offenses.

While technical revocations are a more efficient way to return persons to prison, they are also likely to refill the prison to capacity sooner. Hence, the double bind on the parole officer. Legislation responding to the impact of parole decisions on the increased crowding side of the double bind came in 1985 in the form of Senate Bill (S.B.) 1167. The explicit purpose of this law was to reduce prison crowding due to violations of the administrative conditions of parole. In particular, it allowed prison officials to reinstate good-time credits (after ninety days of satisfactory institutional adjustment) accumulated during the returning individual's previous stay in prison. This resulted in substantially shortened lengths of stay for those returned for technical reasons associated with the violation of the special conditions of parole. Thus, when a person had committed a new crime, there were benefits to the offender in securing a technical revocation rather than a new conviction. In the process, the legislative intent of reducing prison crowding from administrative parole revocation decisions resulted in the aggravation of the revolving-door syndrome of release and return.

In February 1987, the emergency provisions of the PMA were implemented for the first time. Eligible inmates were awarded an extra sixty days, and the prison system was closed to new admissions for twelve days. In the next two months, the doors were closed for a total of seventeen days and eligible inmates were credited with up to ninety extra days. Later this same year, from June through September, new admissions were denied for a total of forty-one days and again eligible inmates had their sentences reduced by up to ninety days. The next ninety-day discounted sentences came in July of 1988. Between September 1988 and March 1989, the prison system refused new admissions for sixteen days.

The Legislature Restructures the Criminal Justice System

This, then, was the situation when the Seventy-first Legislature convened in 1989. The prison system continued to bulge at the seams. The Board of Pardons and Paroles was releasing almost 80 percent of those eligible for parole at their initial hearing. Simultaneously, inmates were being released on sentences shortened by up to three months. Many of these same parolees were being returned on technical violations. With a technical violation, the chance for a second early release was increased. Local jails were filling beyond their capacity, due, in part, to the back pressure from the TDC. Faced with their own economic pressures and jail-crowding lawsuits, local officials began suing the state. Population and crime-rate projections offered little hope for relief in the near future.

In this pressurized economic and political atmosphere, otherwise radical reforms began to look increasingly attractive. Hard-line law-and-order rhetoric gave way to an unprecedented consensus that something different had to be done. The expensive expansion of prison space by itself was not going to be enough. Largely at the initiation of Lieutenant Governor William Hobby, legislation was passed for a wide range of early childhood and adolescent crime-prevention programs. In addition, measures were passed that called for the restructuring of criminal justice agencies while distributing new resources and sentencing alternatives to local authorities.

With very little exaggeration, these measures were hailed as revolutionary departures from conventional wisdom in Texas. To be sure, more funds were appropriated to expand prison capacity. The Seventieth Legislature had approved some $500 million for the funding of nearly 14,000 new TDC beds. In 1989, the Seventy-first Legislature authorized another $400 million in general obligation bonds, subject to voter approval. If financed over twenty years, these latter bonds would cost, according to estimates provided by the Legislative Budget Board, an additional billion dollars.

Taken together, these funding packages would potentially expand the prison capacity by just under 30,000 beds by 1991. This would also mean that Texas would build, in roughly a four-year period, so many new beds that—even without the existing prison system—it would be the sixth largest in the United States. As it turned out the planned expansion would take a little longer, but nevertheless the building plans went forward as the 1990s unfolded.

With one exception, such an ambitious plan was without precedent. California provided the only experience to draw upon. In the early 1980s

California and Texas were exchanging positions as the largest state prison system, with population totals approaching 40,000. California then embarked on an extensive expansion program to the point in 1989 when they were housing over 80,000 inmates. Evidence from a number of sources indicated that even with this generous allocation of public tax dollars to expand prison capacity, cells were being filled faster than they were being built. In a quite pessimistic report to the California Senate Appropriations Committee, the California Department of Corrections lamented that even with some 47,000 new prison beds, by 1994 the prison system would be running at something over 200 percent of capacity (Zimring 1990).

Without regulating sentencing practices, without developing alternatives to incarceration, without devoting funds to programs designed to break the cycle of low income, low education, and a higher probability of crime, the message was clear. Construction programs alone, even very ambitious ones, were not likely to be enough. This message was not lost on the Seventy-first Legislature.

The most important changes stemmed from legislation fashioned and supported by a number of influential legislators in House Bill (H.B.) 2335. Guided by the belief that part of the sentencing problem was a lack of communication and coordination among the components of the criminal justice system, this bill consolidated the Texas Department of Corrections, the Board of Pardons and Paroles, and the Texas Adult Probation Commission under a single umbrella agency. With this more efficient structure in place, additional provisions were aimed at affecting the flow of convicted felons in very specific ways.

Lawyers, judges, and academics had recognized for a number of years that sentence disparity throughout the state meant some jurisdictions were using more than their fair share of prison beds. When the crowding crisis hit full force, TDC officials adopted the policy that beds would be allocated according to past demands. This, of course, meant that traditional "overuse" could continue. With the passage of the new legislation, the Texas Board of Corrections was directed to devise an allocation formula based not on past sentencing practices but on a formula that would include such variables as the uniform crime rate of the state and county (the incidence of violent crime was to be given more weight), the current population and population growth of the county, and a scale for assessing the "risk" of sentenced felons. Once devised and put in place in 1990 with some allowance for ongoing local jail suits, it was hoped that through various incentives and the sanction of allocated space, justice in Texas could be more equitably distributed as implemented through the resource of a prison bed.

With more equitable distribution of prison space and the belief that incarceration alone was not the answer, a more detailed "stairstep" sanction system was enacted through expanded use of risk assessment scales, jail good-time provisions, work-release programs, electronic monitoring, community service, and literacy testing. By any measure these were far-reaching reforms. It remains to be seen whether they will work. As always, much will depend on implementation and on discretionary decisions made at the front end of the system by prosecutors and judges along with parole and probation officers. The remaining chapters will focus on an important portion of these decisions.

In 1988, slightly over 11,000 inmates, out of a total of some 33,000, were admitted to the TDC for violating conditions of parole or mandatory supervision. Much effort has gone into investigating the patterns and correlates of this revocation process. However, relatively little attention has been given to how these patterns and correlates shift in the context of a criminal justice system under extreme pressures for change. It is on this question that the remainder of this book is focused.

The Study Design

Given substantial increases in the number of parole releases and the likely resultant change in the composition of the parolee population, it is important to assess the extent to which reincarceration rates have changed over this time period. The specific question we address is how did this transformation in Texas criminal justice in the 1980s affect recidivism patterns of those released on parole.

The primary analytic strategy is to compare the survival patterns, i.e., reincarceration rates, of four parole cohorts released from the TDC between 1984 and 1987. In addition, we will examine parallel data for cohorts released under the emergency provisions of the PMA. The design is longitudinal, providing for the evaluation over time of inmates released in a given year as well as the assessment of changes across cohorts of parolees. Thus, our focus is on the shifting patterns and overall probabilities of reincarceration during this period of dramatically revised criminal justice policies.

Survival analysis (Brown et al. 1979) is an appropriate analytic method when the variable of interest is the time interval between an initial event (in this case release from prison) and a subsequent, terminal event (reincarceration).

Survival times are measured in monthly intervals, permitting the computation of monthly survival trajectories for each cohort. Two related survival functions used in the analysis are (1) the cumulative proportion surviving at the end of a specified time interval is one minus what is typically treated as the recidivism rate and (2) the hazard rate, or the probability that persons not reincarcerated at the beginning of a specified time interval (month) will be reincarcerated during that interval.

Initially, we will be occupied with whether characteristics of parolees have changed over time. One question to be answered is whether there was a "hardening" of the cohorts and the extent to which this shift in parolee characteristics may have influenced the probability of their being returned to prison, as well as the length of time between release and reincarceration. Special attention will be given to the impact of specific events such as the enactment of the PMA and the subsequent closing of the prison system to admissions.

We will look closely at the survival patterns of persons released to see if these patterns changed over time, whether the points of highest risk of returning to prison shifted as the prison and parole systems adjusted to various pressures, and whether we find any variation in the well-documented "transition curve," wherein persons move from an early period of increasing risk during the first year or so to a later period, wherein the probability of returning to prison becomes progressively less pronounced. Finally, some analytic effort will be spent on validating predictive models for parole success, models that hold even in periods of dramatic pressures from the courts, legislature, and the media.

Records provided by the Texas Board of Pardons and Paroles, the Texas Department of Public Safety, and the Texas Department of Corrections were used to compile data on four cohorts of parolees released in February 1984, 1985, 1986, and 1987. These cohorts consist of 1,435, 1,119, 1,671, and 2,063 parolees respectively. It is important to emphasize that these four cohorts are representative of parolees in general. Comparisons of the characteristics of the sample cohorts with those for all releasees in 1984, 1985, 1986, and 1987 showed essentially no differences.

The research design allows for a thirty-six month follow-up for all four release cohorts with monthly tracking to determine not only if parolees were reincarcerated but also how long after release parolees were returned to prison. In addition, thirty-six month follow-up data were collected on two cohorts of parolees, one of which was released under the emergency provisions of the PMA and another control group of parolees who resemble the PMA releases but who did not receive accelerated release.

Data on the characteristics of parolees include prior incarceration offense (release offense), age, gender, race/ethnicity, assessed risk, region of the state to which persons were released, and reincarceration offense (return offense). Prior incarceration offense and reincarceration offense categories consist of murder, sexual assault, robbery, burglary, larceny/theft, motor vehicle theft, fraud/forgery, drug offenses, assault, and traffic/DWI. For return offenses we also coded technical violations. Age is categorized into 18 to 22, 23 to 27, 28 to 32, 33 to 37, 38 to 42, and 43-plus years. Race/ethnicity includes Anglo, African-American, and Latino. Assessed risk, based on the multidimensional Salient Factor Score (appendix A) was collapsed into high (a score of between 0 and 4), medium (between 5 and 10), and low (11 to 15). Finally, there are ten regions of parole release: Dallas, Houston, San Antonio, Lubbock, Fort Worth, Angleton, Tyler, Waco, El Paso, and Corpus Christi (appendix B).

3
Intra-Cohort Variation in Reincarceration

While the primary focus of this research is the longitudinal analysis of reincarceration patterns across successive cohorts of parolees, it is also important to assess the characteristics and survival patterns of parolees *within* a release cohort. We are interested in two basic questions. First, what are the primary relationships among the characteristics of parolees. Second, are there patterns of reincarceration that depart from previous research that might be linked to changes in the criminal justice system during the years this study examines?

We base our analysis on the pooled 1984 and 1985 release cohorts. We pooled these cohorts for two reasons. First, the analysis requires a relatively large number of parolees. Pooling these cohorts provides the necessary sample size. Second, the statistical evaluation of the probabilities and timing of reincarceration for these two cohorts indicated they were not significantly different from each other ($D = 1.5$, $p = .22$). This overlap is graphically evident in figure 3.1.

Characteristics of the Pooled 1984 and 1985 Cohorts

The pooled 1984–85 release cohort consists of 2,554 individuals, 56 percent of whom were released in 1984 and 44 percent of whom were released in 1985. Figure 3.2 presents the percentage distributions of parolee characteristics including release offense, gender, age, race/ethnicity, assessed risk, region, and reincarceration offense.

In terms of demographic characteristics, the typical parolee was a white male between the ages of twenty-three and twenty-seven. The vast majority of parolees were male (approximately 93 percent). Nearly 45 percent were between the ages of eighteen and twenty-seven. Two-thirds were eighteen to thirty-two years of age. Anglos constituted approximately 42 percent of the cohort. Nearly 40 percent of the parolees were African-American, and 19 percent were Latino.

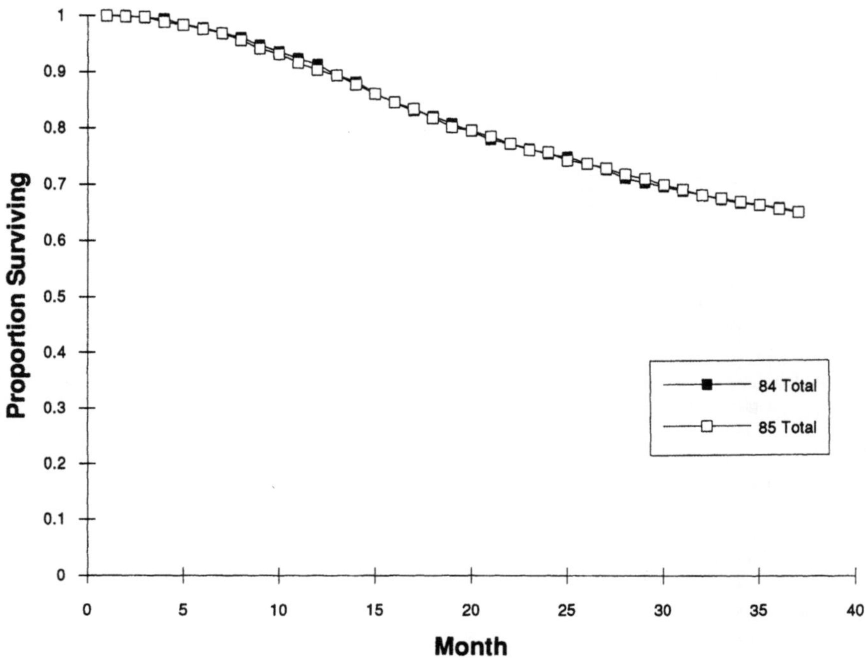

FIGURE 3.1. Survival curves for the 1984 and 1985 cohorts.

This distribution of demographic characteristics is consistent with the distribution among the larger parole population released in these years. It is also fairly representative of the prison population at TDC in 1984 and 1985, though African-Americans comprised a slightly higher percentage of the inmate population (42 percent) and Anglos a slightly lower percentage (37 percent).

Parolees in our sample were likewise similar to the larger parole populations of 1984 and 1985 in terms of the offense for which they had served a prison sentence (release offense). The most common release offense was burglary (30 percent), followed by larceny/theft (15 percent), robbery (13 percent) and drug trafficking offenses (10 percent). The majority of parolees were judged to be of medium risk (62 percent), while almost 11 percent were assessed as high risk and 27 percent as minimum risk.

Individuals released on parole were returned to a variety of jurisdictions throughout the state (appendix B). The majority of parolees were released to the larger urban areas—67 percent of the pooled cohort were released to either the Dallas, Houston, San Antonio, or Fort Worth regions.

The most common reincarceration offense was burglary (23 percent), followed by parole revocation for technical violations (16 percent), drug offenses (10 percent), and larceny (9 percent). Homicide was the least common return offense.

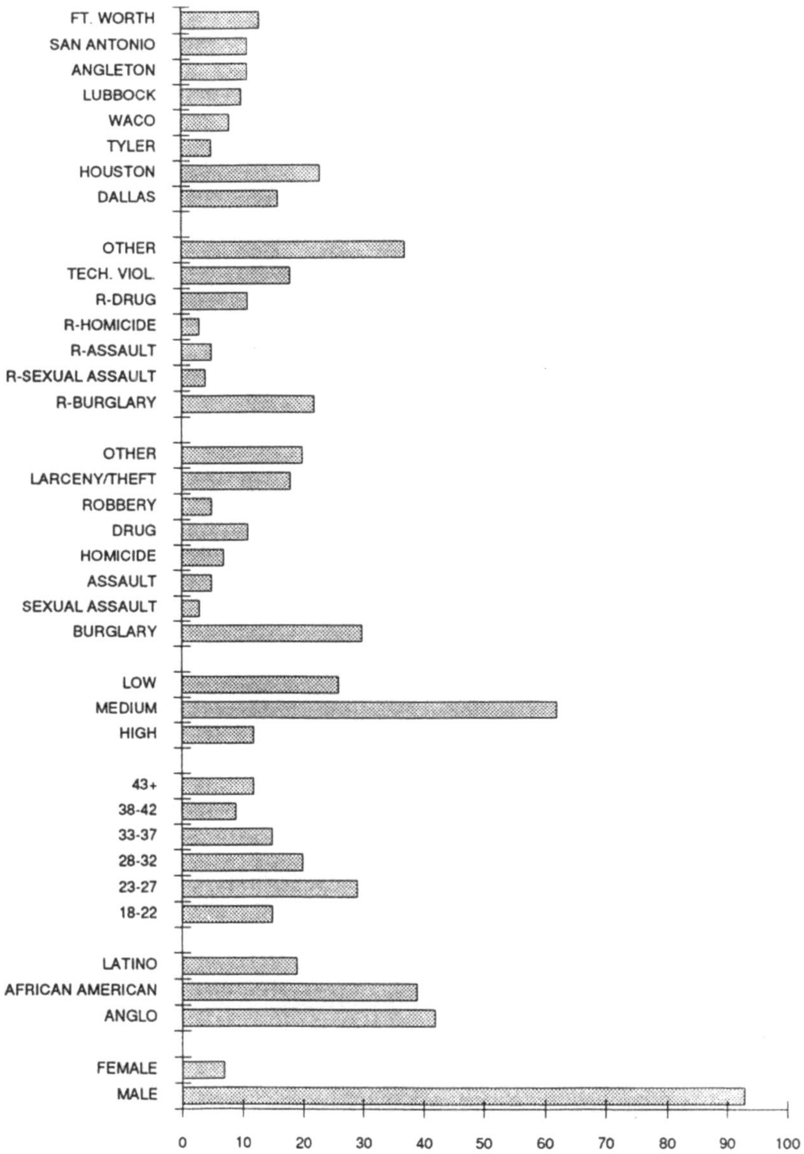

FIGURE 3.2. Composition of pooled 1984–1985 cohorts.

Cross-tabulations of release offense by race/ethnicity, gender, age, risk, and region of release (not presented in tabular form here) indicate a number of statistically significant relationships. Burglary is the most common offense for all three race/ethnic groups, constituting 29 percent of all offenses committed by Anglos and African-Americans and 35 percent of all offenses committed by Latinos. However, differences in offense patterns by race/ethnicity do exist. In particular, African-Americans are overrepresented in the robbery and assault categories. Anglos are more likely to have been incarcerated for motor vehicle theft (MVT) and Latinos for homicide, assault, and drug offenses. Conversely, African-Americans are much less likely to have been in prison for traffic/DWI and drugs, while Anglos are disproportionately less likely to have prison sentences for assault and robbery. Finally, Latino parolees tend to be underrepresented in the offense categories of larceny/theft, MVT, and forgery/fraud.

The differentials by gender are predictable. The modal offense for males is burglary, and for females it is larceny/theft. Proportionately, females are more likely to have been incarcerated for forgery/fraud and trafficking in drugs. Finally, there is also a slight overrepresentation of females released after serving a sentence for homicide.

Burglary is the most common release offense for all age groups with the exception of parolees forty-three years of age and older. For this older group, larceny/theft is the most common, followed by homicide. There is, however, variation in release offense across age categories. The youngest parolees (eighteen to twenty-two) are disproportionately more likely to have been incarcerated for property offenses, especially burglary and MVT. Parolees in the twenty-three to twenty-seven age group have similar prior incarceration offenses, except they are also more likely to have prison sentences for robbery. The pattern changes for the twenty-eight to thirty-two year age group. These individuals are more likely to have forgery/fraud and drug trafficking release offenses. Finally, the forty-three-plus age group is heavily overrepresented among those with prison time for homicide and traffic/DWI.

Property crimes are the most common among those assessed as high- or medium-risk parolees, while violent release offenses constitute the modal category for those assessed as minimum-risk offenders. More specifically, burglary and larceny/theft constitute 60 percent of the release offense for the high-risk group and nearly 50 percent for the medium-risk group. On the other hand, burglary and larceny comprise only 29 percent of the offenses for minimum-risk releasees. Among low-risk parolees, 31 percent had been in prison for robbery and homicide, with an additional 13 percent incarcerated for drug offenses. Thus, it should be emphasized that the risk score is assessed mainly in terms of probable recidivism rather than on the severity of a previous offense.

Differences in release offense are less dramatic by region when compared to the other characteristics. Property offenses, in particular burglary, are the most common. However, there is a slight tendency for violent offenses to be overrepresented among parolees released to Dallas and San Antonio, but underrepresented among those in Lubbock and Fort Worth. Moreover, while slight, parolees in the Lubbock and Angleton regions are disproportionately more likely to have been in prison for drug trafficking offenses. The opposite is the case for those in Dallas and Tyler.

Cross-tabulations of parolee characteristics by *return offense* also are statistically significant. Burglary is the most common reincarceration offense among all three race/ethnic groups with the exception of Anglos, for whom burglary and technical violations are equally common. African-American parolees have a disproportionately higher likelihood of being reincarcerated for violent offenses, specifically robbery and assault, as well as larceny. African-Americans were less likely to return for MVT, traffic offenses, and technical violations. Anglos are more likely to return to prison for sexual assault, MVT, traffic offenses, and technical violations and are less likely to be reincarcerated for robbery, assault, and larceny. Latino parolees are overrepresented in the homicide category, traffic/DWI, and assault. They are less likely to return for sexual assault, robbery, larceny, forgery, and drug offenses.

The pattern by gender is largely similar to that for prior incarceration offenses. The modal female return offense was forgery/fraud, followed by technical violations. Burglary was the most common offense among males.

The most common return offense by age was burglary for the four younger age groups (18 to 22, 23 to 27, 28 to 32, and 33 to 37). Technical violation was the most common for the thirty-eight to forty-two and forty-three-plus age groups. The youngest age group was more likely to return for burglary and MVT. Finally, the two oldest age groups were more likely to return for traffic/DWI convictions when compared to other age groups.

Once again, burglary is the modal return offense for high- and medium-risk parolees. However, technical violations are the most common for the low-risk group. Parolees assessed as high risk are overrepresented in the burglary category while those assessed as medium risk are more likely to return for murder and robbery. Low-risk parolees have a higher likelihood of reincarceration for sexual assault and drug offenses.

Technical violations were the most common reason to return to prison in two of the release regions—Lubbock and Angleton. Burglary was the most common return offense in the remaining regions. There was no consistent pattern with regard to disproportionately higher or lower probabilities by region. Sexual assault had a higher probability in Dallas; MVT and drug offenses in Houston; traffic/DWI in San Antonio; traffic/DWI and technical violations in Lubbock; fraud in Fort Worth; technical violations in Angleton; homicide in Tyler; and assault in Waco.

There is a significant, although weak, relationship between race/ethnicity and gender, with women overrepresented among African-American parolees and underrepresented among Latinos, and, to a lesser extent, among Anglos. A similarly statistically significant but weak relationship exists between race/ethnicity and age. There are proportionally more Latinos in the 18 to 22 age group and more African-Americans in the twenty-eight to thirty-two and thirty-three to thirty-seven age groups. Finally, African-Americans tend to be underrepresented among those forty-three and older. There is no relationship between race/ethnicity and assessed risk.

The relationship between race/ethnicity and region of release is significant and a bit stronger than those just discussed. African-American parolees tend to be overrepresented in the Dallas, Houston, Angleton, and Tyler parole regions of the state, while Anglos constitute a relatively large proportion of those released to Fort Worth and Tyler. Latinos are disproportionately concentrated in the San Antonio–South Texas region. Each of these findings corresponds to ethnic populations throughout the state.

The gender-assessed risk relationship is the only significant one involving gender, and it is as would be expected. Males tend to be disproportionately concentrated in the high-risk category and females in the low-risk group.

There is no significant relationship between age and region or assessed risk and region. However, assessed risk and age are related, though not linearly. Approximately 70 percent of the medium-risk groups and 62 percent of the low-risk groups consist of parolees under the age of thirty-three. About 53 percent of those assessed as high risk are under age thirty-three. The high-risk category is overrepresented by parolees thirty-eight and older, while those from eighteen to twenty-two are disproportionately more likely to be assessed as medium risk. There is also a tendency for the age forty-three and older parolees to be overrepresented in the low-risk category.

While reporting these relationships sounds much like a litany of well-established previous findings, it is important to keep them in mind as we progress into the analyses in later chapters. It is also important to note that the massive changes taking place in Texas criminal justice during this time had little or no apparent impact on the basic characteristics of parolees in these early cohorts. Thus, these findings can serve as baseline data to be used when assessing changes in parolee characteristics and patterns of reincarceration among later cohorts.

Overall Reincarceration Rates

Figure 3.3 presents the month-to-month survival probabilities for the pooled cohorts for a follow-up period of thirty-six months. While there is some fluctuation, the trend in the survival rates indicates a fairly steady decline in parole success. About seven months after release, the cumulative proportion of survivors declines relatively steadily and then begins to level off at about thirty-two months. It is important to note that the combination of these two cohorts does not produce any distortion in the survival trends since the patterns are essentially identical for the 1984 and 1985 parolees.

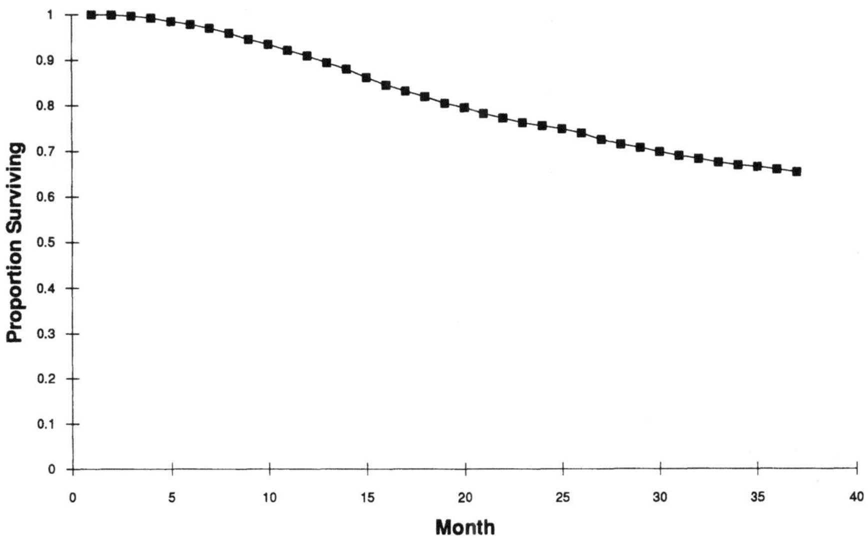

FIGURE 3.3. Survival curve for total pooled cohort.

Figure 3.4 charts the six-month moving averages of the hazard rates over the same thirty-six month period of observation. The hazard rates increase nearly monotonically from the first month of release up to the fifteenth month, where the rate peaks. The rates then decline fairly

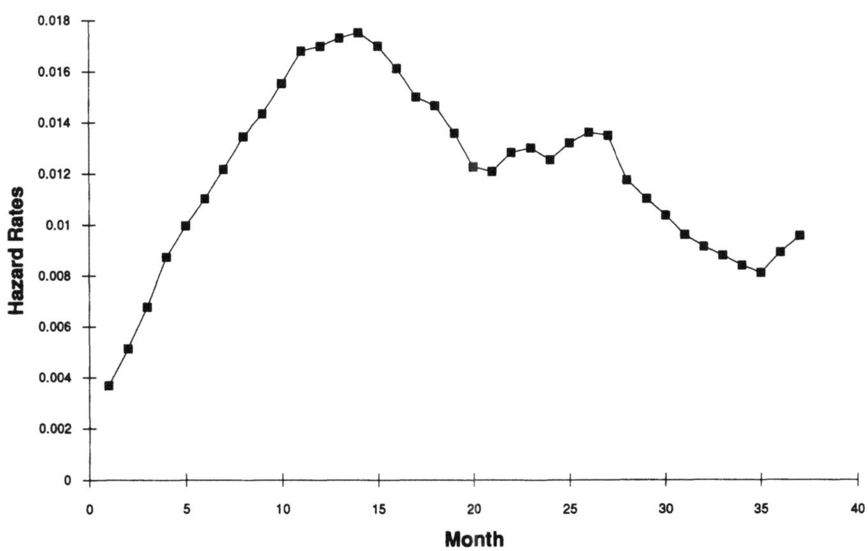

FIGURE 3.4. Hazard rates for total pooled cohort.

steadily from the fifteenth month to the twenty-first month, where they level off somewhat for a period of a few months. There is then a decline which counterbalances the earlier period of increase.

This pattern in hazard rates reconfirms the idea that there is an important transition period shortly after release, during which the probability of reinvolvement in criminal activity is heightened. Numerous studies have suggested that the difficulty of this transition and thus the shape of

TABLE 3.1. Survival probabilities for the pooled 1984–85 release cohort.

	12 Months	24 Months	36 Months
Total	89.4	74.8	65.2
Release Offense			
Murder	92.3	83.9	76.8
Rape	93.2	76.3	61.0
Robbery	90.3	74.4	62.3
Burglary	85.3	66.8	56.7
Larceny	89.3	77.2	70.4
MVT	83.6	63.8	50.0
Forgery	91.5	78.0	70.0
Drug	97.2	85.8	74.4
Assault	91.9	77.8	73.7
Traffic/DWI	90.0	80.0	72.2
Gender			
Male	89.0	74.0	64.0
Female	95.2	85.0	80.7
Age			
18–22	85.0	66.2	55.9
23–27	88.7	74.5	64.9
28–32	91.6	74.1	62.8
33–37	90.5	77.7	69.5
38–42	91.6	75.4	65.6
43+	89.4	83.0	76.3
Race/Ethnicity			
Anglo	91.0	78.5	71.0
African-American	87.5	70.7	60.4
Latino	90.1	74.9	62.5
Risk			
High	80.8	61.0	50.0
Medium	88.7	73.3	62.9
Low	94.6	84.0	76.9
Region			
Dallas	87.3	72.8	63.0
Houston	89.0	74.6	64.3
San Antonio	86.9	70.4	59.2
Lubbock	91.3	70.9	57.7
Fort Worth	90.8	76.8	68.3
Angleton	90.7	73.2	64.2
Tyler	86.9	73.8	64.8
Waco	85.3	68.9	62.3

the hazard rate curve is linked to the psychological condition called *post-release depression*, as well as the availability of supportive networks and the probability of employment upon release (e.g., Bureau of Justice Statistics 1984; Ekland-Olson et al. 1983; Rossi et al. 1980; Irwin 1970). Basically, if individuals make it past the early post-release "hump," the chances of their returning to prison decline dramatically.

It is important to keep in mind that our definition of recidivism is reincarceration. The hazard rates and survival probabilities for rearrest and conviction would be different. Specifically, for rearrest the hazard rates would be higher and would increase more rapidly in the early period after release. Moreover, the survival curves would decline more rapidly, resulting in lower survival probabilities at any given interval. For example, a Bureau of Justice Statistics report (1989) indicated that 25 percent of a national sample of inmates released in 1983 had been rearrested at the end of six months following release. After one year, 39 percent had been rearrested, 23 percent convicted, and 19 percent reincarcerated. The three-year figures are 62 percent, 47 percent, and 41 percent respectively.

Table 3.1 presents the cumulative percent surviving at twelve, twenty-four, and thirty-six month intervals for the pooled sample. The table is broken down by the characteristics of release offense, gender, age, race/ethnicity, assessed risk, and region of release. After twelve months, over 10 percent of the total parole sample had been reincarcerated. That increased to 25 percent after twenty-four months of release and nearly 35 percent after thirty-six months.

The three-year return rate for these parolees in Texas is comparable with national data (Bureau of Justice Statistics 1989). In the national study, the overall reincarceration rate was slightly higher for 1983 releasees compared to those in our sample. Based on data from eleven states, representing over one-half of the number of persons released nationally, the Bureau of Justice Statistics study reported a three-year reincarceration rate of 41 percent. These national data included jail sentences as well as reincarceration in prison. Allowing for this difference, as well as the fact that the national data reported criminal activity data both within and outside the states in which the inmates were released, the two sets of data are quite consistent.

Differential Reincarceration Rates

Our analysis of intra-cohort variation in the probability of returning to prison is based on the assessment of the extent to which reincarceration is a function of demographic characteristics, original incarceration offense, assessed risk at time of release, and the region of the state to which parolees returned.

The most consistent finding, one that has been called a brutal fact (Hirschi and Gottfredson 1983), is the link between age and involvement

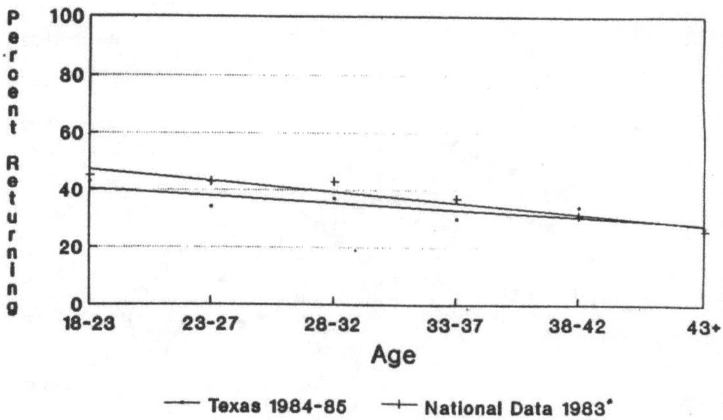

FIGURE 3.5. Returned to prison after three years (age at release). Age categories in national study were 18–24, 25–29, 30–34, 35–39, 40–44, 45+.

in crime. This relationship is once again confirmed among the parolees released from the Texas Department of Corrections in 1984 and 1985. The detailed trend data along with roughly comparable national data are reported in figure 3.5. At the two extremes, 43 percent of those persons between the ages of eighteen and twenty-three at time of release had returned to prison three years after release, compared to 23 percent of those who were forty-three years of age or older. The *D* statistic across all age groups is statistically significant ($D = 32.9, p = .000$).

Figures 3.6 and 3.7 present the trends in hazard rates by age. All of the age categories exhibit similar patterns during the early months after release (the first ten to twelve months), a period where the rates increase rapidly. The rates for age groups from 18 to 22, 28 to 32, and 38 to 42 have a second peak in the early part of the third year. The 23 to 27 and 43-plus age categories experience the initial peak, but then gradually decline throughout the remainder of the release period.

It has been reported repeatedly—in findings similar to those linking age and criminal activity—that males are more involved in criminal activities than females, though in recent years some narrowing of the gap has been noted. Among the 1984–85 parolees in Texas this, too, is reconfirmed. At the end of three years after release, 35 percent of the males had returned to prison, whereas only 18 percent of the females once again found themselves back in the prison cell block. This difference in the cumulative percent surviving by gender is statistically significant ($D = 21.4, p = .000$).

More specifically, the failure rate for males increases at a faster rate as the length of release increases. This is indicated by computing the ratio of

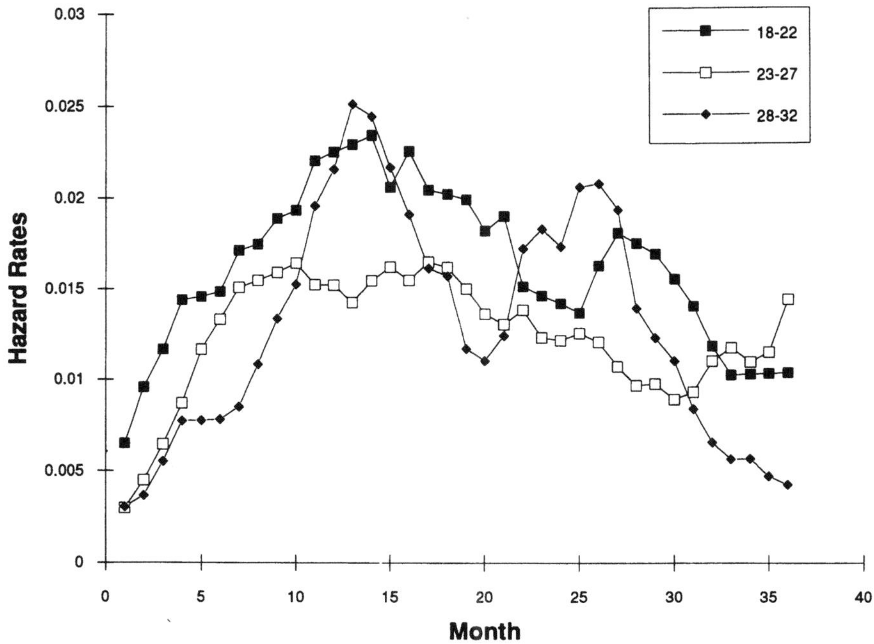

FIGURE 3.6. Hazard rates by age—pooled cohort.

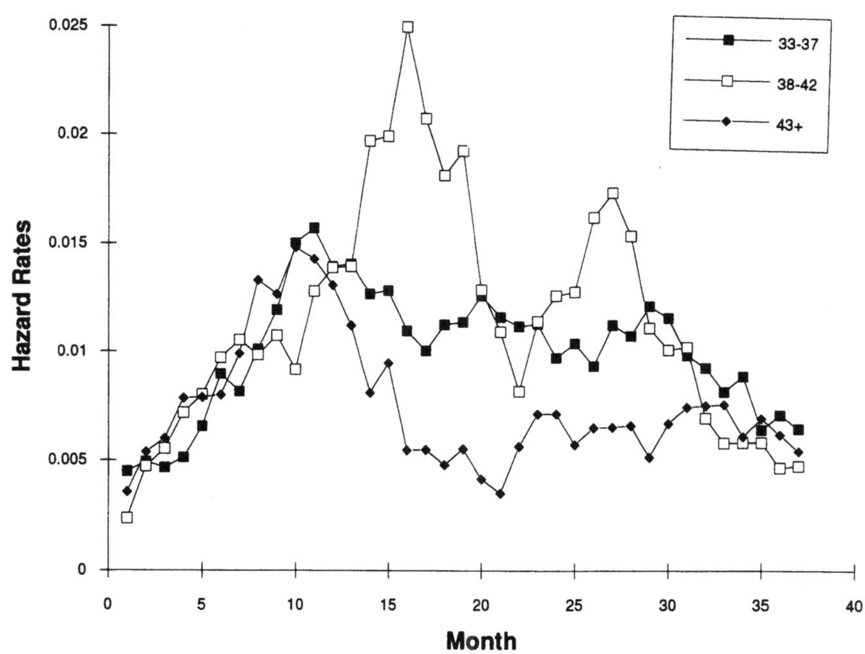

FIGURE 3.7. Hazard rates by age—pooled cohort.

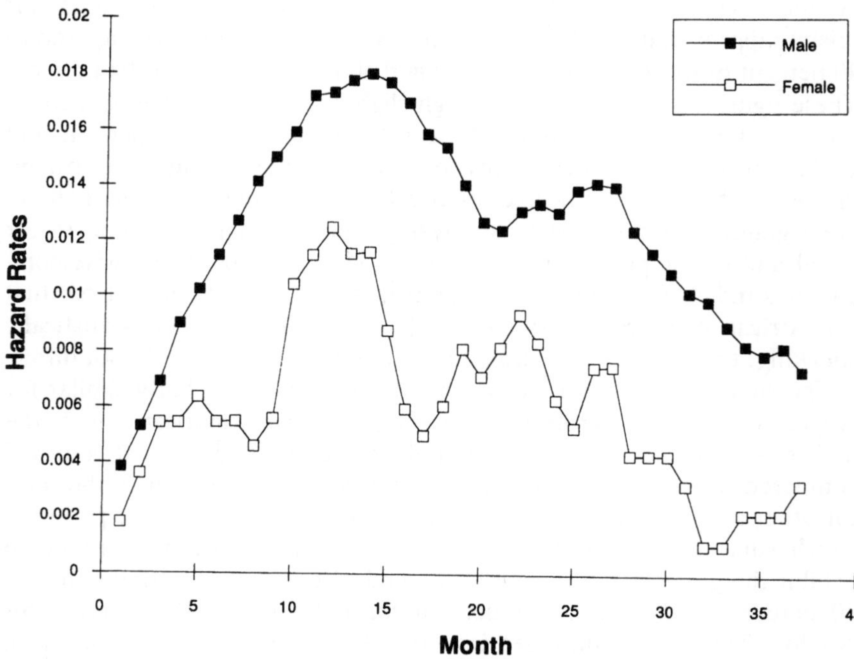

FIGURE 3.8. Hazard rates by gender—pooled cohort.

the male survival rate to that for females. After twelve months, the survival rate for males is 93 percent of that for females. After twenty-four months it is 87 percent, and then drops to 79 percent by thirty-six months.

This failure rate difference is reflected in the respective hazard rates (figure 3.8). The rates for males increase relatively steadily from the first month of release to approximately the fifteenth month, then decline for about seven months, rise again slightly for six months, and then decline throughout the remainder of the release period. Among females, not only are the hazard rates lower, they increase more slowly in the early months (the first nine months), peak earlier at about the twelfth month, and then decline gradually with some minor fluctuations.

The difference in the reincarceration rates for males and females in Texas appears to be greater than in other states. In Texas, the return rates for males is about twice that for females. Data reported by the Bureau of Justice Statistics (1989) indicate that males are more likely to be reincarcerated than females, but the difference is not as dramatic (42 percent for males compared to 33 percent for females). However, this difference might be due to variance in criteria for reincarceration across these studies.

Less dramatic, though still consistent with previous research, are the differences found among persons from different racial and ethnic backgrounds. Three years after the Texas parolees we followed had left prison, approximately 30 percent of the Anglos had returned compared to 40 percent of the African-Americans and about 38 percent of the Latinos. These figures, are parallel to, though slightly lower than, national totals reported for the 1983 cohort (African-Americans were 45 percent and Latinos were 47 percent; figures for whites, which include Latinos, indicated a three-year reincarceration rate of 38 percent). Overall, there are significant differences in survival patterns among the three major racial and ethnic groups in Texas ($D = 34.5$, $p = .000$). Pairwise comparisons indicate that the Anglo survival trajectory is different from that for African-Americans and Latinos ($p < .000$). However, statistically speaking, the African-American and Latino survival curves do not differ.

The survival rates after twelve months of release are fairly similar for Anglo and Latino parolees (table 3.1). African-Americans have the highest failure rate during this period of release (12.5 percent returned compared to 10.5 percent for the total sample). Consistent with the rates for other subgroups, the second twelve months of release is the period in which survival rates decline the most. African-Americans continue to exhibit the greatest return rate at the end of twenty-four months (nearly 30 percent) compared to 25 percent for Latinos and 21.5 percent for Anglos. This trend continues into the third year of release, in which nearly 40 percent of African-American and 38 percent of Latino parolees are returned. The survival rate for Anglos declines relatively less compared to those of the other groups. Finally, the survival probabilities for African-Americans and Latinos appear to converge as time of release increases.

Figure 3.9 presents the trends in the hazard rates for the three racial and ethnic categories. The post-release transition period is apparent in all three racial and ethnic groups. The rates for all three groups increase rather rapidly during the early months of release (approximately the first eight months). A leveling off occurs at approximately the same time for all three groups; however, the rates for African-Americans and Latinos are considerably higher than those for Anglos. After the leveling off period at about fifteen months, the Anglo rates decline nearly monotonically and essentially level off again after the thirty-first or thirty-second month of release. The African-American rates decline somewhat after the fifteenth month, fluctuate for a period of time, and then decline dramatically during most of the third year. The Latino hazard rates reveal a different trend. While dropping during the middle of the second year, there appears to be a second hump in the early part of the third year. Unlike the African-American rates, those for Latino parolees appear to level off sooner and at a higher level.

Over the past several decades, much effort has been expended to explain this variation across members of majority and minority groups. These explanations (e.g., Wilson 1987) have ranged from speculations

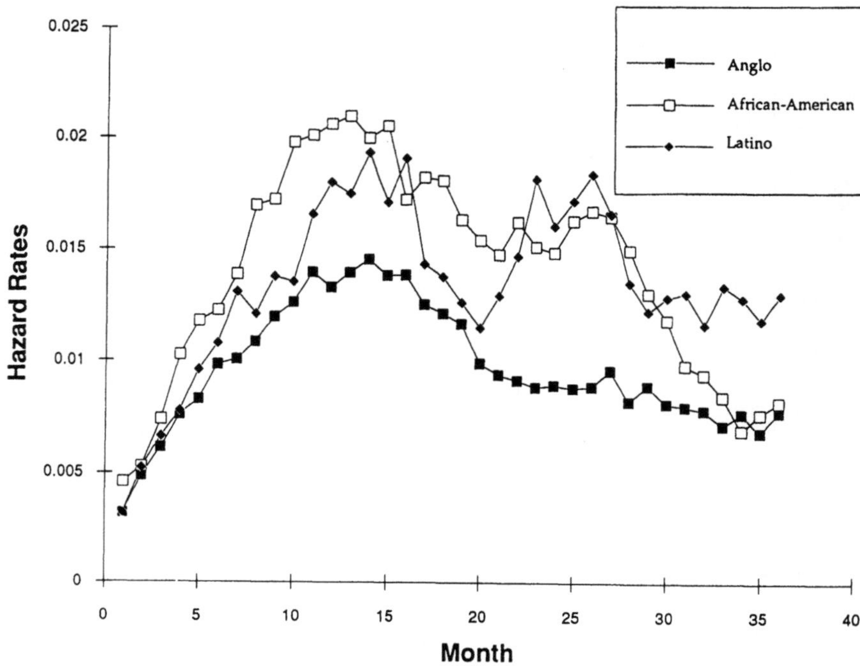

FIGURE 3.9. Hazard rates by race ethnicity—pooled cohort.

about subcultures to suppositions concerning the importance of educational levels, family values, and stability, and most recently to the significance of historical patterns of discrimination in the production of an isolated underclass of the "truly disadvantaged." We will turn to analyses relevant to some of these explanations in chapter 5.

Beyond age, gender, and race/ethnicity, there is less consistency in the literature regarding the relation of personal characteristics to variation in criminal activity (figure 3.10). One factor frequently mentioned is the crime for which persons are incarcerated. It is frequently noted that persons convicted of homicide, taken as a group, constitute a low-risk category when it comes to recidivism. This is sometimes explained by noting that persons convicted of homicide are often not deeply involved in a criminal way of life, but, in a moment of temporary passion, they killed a spouse, friend, or acquaintance.

Whatever the reason, this pattern is replicated in our study of parolees released in 1984 and 1985. Figure 3.11A presents the graphic summary. Persons who were released after serving a sentence for homicide were the least likely to return to prison—23 percent had done so after three years. Persons who had been released after serving a sentence for motor vehicle theft were the most likely to return—49 percent were back in prison after

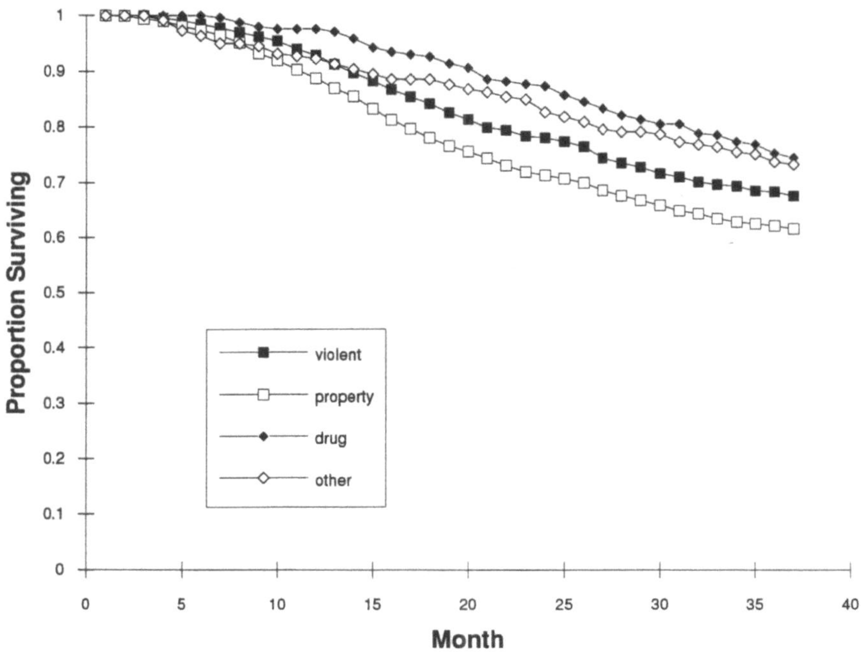

FIGURE 3.10. Survival curves for pooled cohort-P.I.O.

three years. Persons convicted of assault, sexual assault, robbery, and burglary fell in between. The month-to-month survival trajectories for these release offenses are significantly different as a whole ($D = 86.5$, $p = .000$). Comparison of these patterns with the national data such as those contained in figure 3.11B (Bureau of Justice Statistics 1984, 1989), reveals striking similarities.

The trends in the hazard rates for the collapsed offense categories of violent (homicide, sexual assault, robbery, and assault), property (burglary, larceny/theft, fraud/forgery and MVT), and drug offenses are presented in figure 3.12. The hazard rate trends for property and violent offenders are most similar to the pattern for the total sample. The rates for both property and violent offenders increase steadily and peak around fifteen months and then decline for the most part throughout the remainder of the release period. The rates for drug trafficking offenders increase much more gradually and do not exhibit the peak characteristic of the other offense categories.

As in most such matters, the interpretation of these findings is not altogether clear. Persons convicted of homicide are going to serve longer sentences, as a rule, than persons convicted of burglary or auto theft. For this and other reasons, they will be older when they leave prison. For example, 33 percent of those paroled after a sentence for a homicide

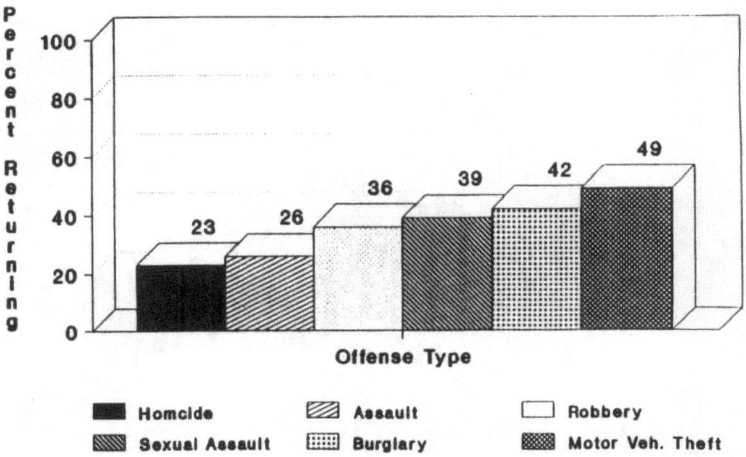

FIGURE 3.11A. Returned to prison after three years (incarceration offense: Texas data).

conviction were in the forty-three or older category as compared to 4, 5, and 8 percent of those paroled after sentences for robbery, burglary, and motor vehicle theft respectively.

We have already noted the close link between age and recidivism in this and other studies. Thus, some caution should be exercised before we conclude that persons convicted of homicide are good parole risks. Instead, they may simply become better parole risks as they mature and serve out

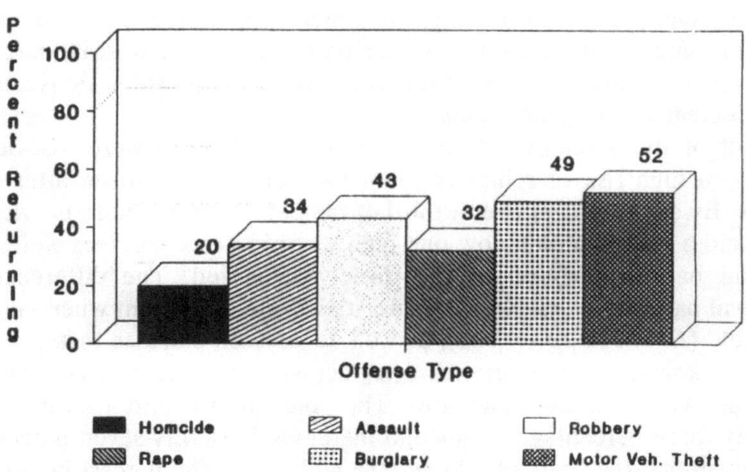

FIGURE 3.11B. Returned to prison after three years (incarceration offense: national data).

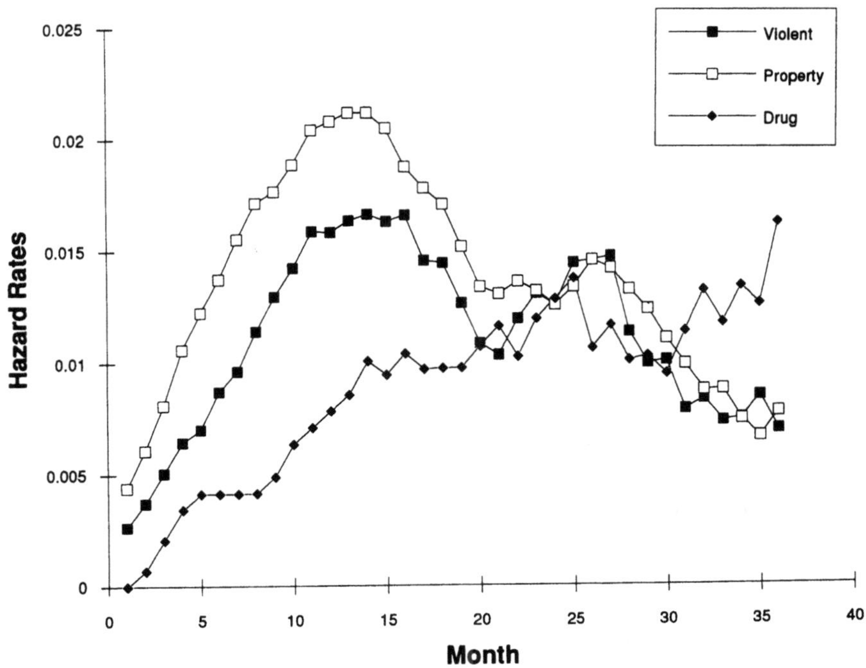

FIGURE 3.12. Hazard rates by release offense—pooled cohort.

their sentence in prison. Before any interpretative conclusions are drawn, we need to look at the data more thoroughly.

In an attempt to take into account a number of predictive factors before releasing persons on parole, members of the Texas Board of Pardons and Paroles looked at scores on the assessed risk scale described in chapter 2. Three years after release, it appears that the scale is a useful supplement for decision making.

Half of those released from prison on parole who were assessed as having a high risk of reincarceration had returned to prison after three years. By contrast, just over a third of the parolees thought to be medium risk and a comparatively low one-quarter of low-risk parolees were back behind bars at the end of the three-year period. The differences in survival patterns by assessed risk are statistically significant when taken as a whole ($D = 93.0$, $p = .000$), as well as for each pairwise test.

The variation in the survival rates across risk categories continues to increase as release time increases. The range after twenty-four months is twenty-three percentage points and increases to twenty-seven percentage points after three years of release (see table 3.1). The highest failure rate for any subgroup is among high-risk parolees. This is the case at all three intervals of release.

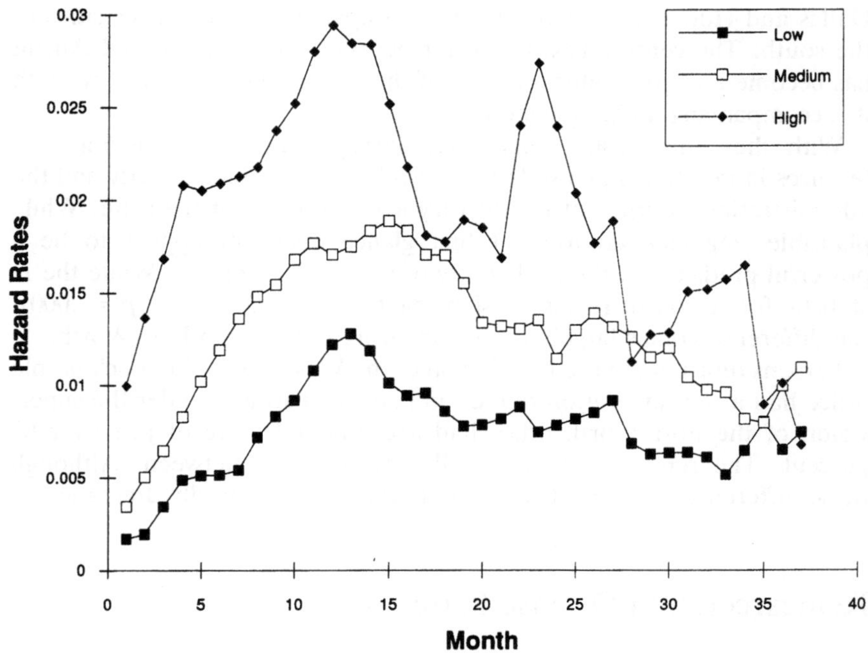

FIGURE 3.13. Hazard rates by risk—pooled cohort.

The trend in the hazard rates by risk (figure 3.13) is quite similar for the medium- and low-risk groups. Both accelerate at about the same rate during the first twelve to thirteen months and then peak. Thereafter, the rates decline relatively steadily. The major difference between these groups is the level of the hazard rates—somewhat higher for the medium risk group. On the other hand, the trend for the high-risk group is quite different from the others. The rates increase more quickly during the first year, peak at a much higher level, decline quickly, and then peak again at the end of the second year. The hazard rates decline through the early part of the third year of release, increase again, and then drop at the end of the third year.

A final set of comparisons can be made regarding the region of the state to which parolees returned. It is sometimes noted that persons return to prison more or less frequently depending on the living conditions in their community. Given the state's reputation, it hardly needs to be noted that Texas is a large and quite diverse state. The rich, piney blackland areas in the eastern part of the state, where plantation farming dominated local economies for many years, are far removed in geography and tradition from the drier plains regions surrounding Midland-Odessa and Lubbock. The cities of El Paso and San Antonio as well as the metropolitan areas of the Lower Rio Grande Valley are mostly Latino.

Dallas and Houston are economic worlds apart from their sister cities to the south. The central Texas corridor between San Antonio and Austin has become a major center for state-of-the-art computer technology, with its accompanying higher paying jobs.

With these historical, geographic, demographic, and economic differences in mind, it is plausible that correlates of criminal activity and the administration of criminal justice vary across regions of the state. While plausible, regional variation at first glance does not appear to be a powerful predictor of the probability of returning to prison. While the D statistic for region of release is significant overall ($D = 81.4$, $p = .000$), the difference comes largely from comparing Lubbock to Fort Worth.

Persons returning to the jurisdiction of the West Texas–Lubbock parole office had a reincarceration rate of 58 percent. Parolees under the supervision of the Fort Worth office had a comparable rate of just over 68 percent. The remaining regions fell somewhere in between. Although these differences are statistically significant, they are hardly dramatic.

Reincarceration Offense Patterns

By the time we stopped collecting information, there were just under one thousand parolees from the pooled 1984–85 cohort of parolees who found themselves back in Texas Department of Corrections institutions. The offenses for which they returned were distributed much like the offenses for which they had been serving time prior to parole. In some instances it is not possible to determine the exact nature of the return offense since returning inmates were often not officially convicted of a new offense, but were returned with the charge of a technical parole violation.

The overall pattern of release and return offenses is presented in table 3.2. Two out of the 155 persons on parole after serving time for homicide were reconvicted for a second homicide charge. Approximately twenty-five of these homicide-convicted parolees were returned to prison for violating some condition of parole. Paroled burglars and those convicted of drug charges were the most consistent group in their criminal activity, with a little over a third of both groups returning to prison for a repeat charge involving drugs or burglary. It is also true that persons who originally went to prison for a property-related offense were generally likely to stick with property-related offenses. Once again, this pattern of repetitious criminal activity is consistent with previous research, though the percentage of persons reconvicted for a second drug dealing or possession charge in the 1989 Bureau of Justice Statistics study was a bit lower (25 percent) than the pattern we found among Texas parolees. These patterns will be explored in greater detail in the next chapter.

TABLE 3.2. Offense patterns of those who returned to prison.

Release Offense	Return Offense: Homicide	Sexual assault	Robbery	Burglary	Larceny theft	MVT	Forgery fraud	Drug sale/poss	Tech. viol.	Total returned
Homicide	5.0	5.0	7.3	7.3	0.0	0.0	5.0	7.3	29.3	41
Sexual assault	0.0	26.9	3.8	3.8	3.8	0.0	3.8	7.7	23.1	26
Robbery	3.4	4.7	20.9	18.2	8.8	1.4	2.0	7.4	14.2	148
Burglary	2.4	3.8	6.5	34.9	6.5	7.3	4.3	6.8	15.4	370
Larceny theft	0.0	1.7	7.4	18.2	22.3	7.8	10.1	9.1	16.5	121
Mo. veh. theft	0.0	0.0	6.3	34.4	7.8	18.8	3.1	10.9	15.6	64
Forgery fraud	2.9	0.0	2.9	18.8	10.1	7.2	26.1	11.6	14.5	69
Drug sale/poss.	2.6	5.2	10.4	7.8	9.1	1.3	3.9	37.7	3.9	77

Conclusion

The motivation for doing this research was to see if the court-induced changes in the administration of criminal justice in Texas in the 1980s had any impact on the probability that persons released on parole would return to prison.

There is no question that the entire criminal justice system in Texas, from arrest to release, was affected by the issue of prison crowding and by court-imposed caps on the prison population. The number of persons released annually increased from 11,000 to 38,000 between 1979 and 1990. The percentage of sentences served moved from an average of 35 percent to an average of 20 percent. Case loads for parole officers increased by about 50 percent. The percentage of persons being released at their initial hearing moved from about 40 percent in 1983 to approximately 80 percent in the late 1980s.

In response to these pressures and the assumption that justice was somehow being damaged in the process, the Texas legislature appropriated funds for expanded prison space that by 1989 added up to approximately a billion dollars in construction costs and an *increase* in yearly operating costs approaching $400 million. The question becomes, Are these funds well spent? There are a number of answers to this question depending on whether the major concern is simple incapacitation, some form of retribution, or a more calculated purpose of deterrence.

Whatever else they imply, changes in the administration of criminal justice in Texas during the period of our research provided an opportunity for a natural experiment: Did the apparent reduction in time served and the escalation in the probability of being released from prison on parole have any impact on the probability that, once released. persons would return more rapidly or with higher eventual probabilities? We conclude that the answer to both of these questions, based on *intra*-cohort comparisons within the pooled 1984–85 cohorts is no.

This conclusion is based on the following findings:

1. There was nothing unusual about the pooled 1984–85 Texas cohort of parolees in terms of individual characteristics or offenses committed.
2. Commonly found correlates of recidivism were reconfirmed.
3. The patterns and probabilities of returning to prison after three years paralleled a Bureau of Justice Statistics study of a 1983 national cohort of persons released from prison as well as numerous previously reported findings.
4. The patterns of return were parallel to the frequently reported transition period across all subgroups of parolees.
5. There were no sharp shifts in recidivism patterns that matched events occurring in the reorganization of the criminal justice system in Texas during this time period.

It should be remembered that while no apparent changes in the specific recidivism patterns of persons released on parole between 1984 and 1985 were detected, it is still possible that changes occurred in subsequent cohorts. To explore this possibility, the next chapter will examine *inter*-cohort differences, including data from subsequent cohorts of parolees.

4
Inter-Cohort Comparisons of Reincarceration Rates

The specific question addressed in this chapter is, "How did the transformation of Texas criminal justice in the 1980s, a period when the burgeoning prison population led to a dramatically expanded use of parole, affect recidivism patterns of successive yearly cohorts of parolees released between 1984 and 1987?" The primary analytic strategy is once again analysis of survival patterns and hazard rates.

At least four mechanisms have been suggested for how the increasing use of parole to regulate the prison population might affect reincarceration rates. The first will be labeled the *composition* explanation. As the number of parole releases increases, the composition of the parole-eligible population changes. For example, the pool of parolees may become increasingly high-risk. This change alone might account for any noted shift in the pattern or probability of returning to prison. The second explanation will be referred to as the *strained resources* argument. The shear volume of parole releases might affect the ability of parole officers to monitor releasees. For example, in 1982, the average case load per parole officer was sixty-seven. By 1986, it had risen to ninety-three parolees per officer. It then declined to ninety in 1987, seventy-two in 1989, and then rose back up to eighty-two in 1990. The third explanation concerns the increasing use of parole, along with related changes in the processing of criminal cases, that may alter the *deterrent* effect of punishment. Fear of punishment, the central variable in deterrence theory, has been found to be linked to the perceived certainty and severity of punishment (Gibbs 1975; Ekland-Olson, et al. 1984). As prisons become crowded, prison officials become more liberal in awarding good-time credits, and as parole boards become increasingly likely to release inmates, the perception of the severity and certainty of imprisonment may decline and with it the deterrent effect of punishment.

The fourth explanation is what will be called the *administrative discretion* influence. Reincarceration rates may reflect changing practices on the part of the parole board and parole officers. Revocation of parole for a technical violation is the decision for which parole officers have the widest discretion. It is reasonable to assume that technical parole violation revocations are most likely to be used on releasees with the most serious criminal records, providing a means for keeping high-risk offenders off the streets without a large investment in court time. Pressure from the media, the legislature, or both may have altered the revocation practices of parole officers by providing a quick and procedurally simpler means for controlling the parole population. As a result, as the proportion of high-risk parolees increases, we might expect to observe increases in technical violation revocations.

Trends in Reincarceration

Figure 4.1 presents the monthly survival probabilities for the thirty-six month follow-up periods for the four cohorts. Two parallel trends are evident. First, as discovered in chapter 3, the 1984 and 1985 cohorts are virtually identical. Second, the trends in the survival probabilities for the 1986 and 1987 cohorts also track one another, although there are some important differences between these latter two groups. Approximately

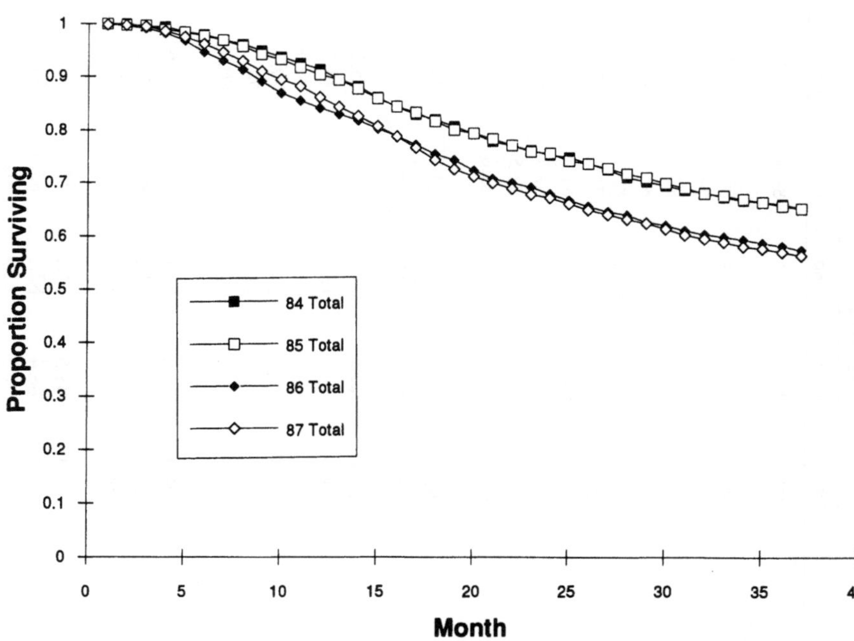

FIGURE 4.1. Cumulative proportion surviving for the 1984–1987 release cohorts: total. Reproduced with permission from Kelly and Ekland-Olson, "The Response of the Criminal Justice System to Prison Overcrowding." *Law and Society Review*, Vol. 25, No. 3: 601–20, 1991. © Law & Society Association.

TABLE 4.1. Survival probabilities for the 1984–87 release cohorts.

	12 Months				24 Months				36 Months			
	1984	1985	1986	1987	1984	1985	1986	1987	1984	1985	1986	1987
Total	89.5	89.4	83.1	84.4	74.9	74.3	66.9	66.2	65.3	65.2	57.5	56.4
Release offense												
Murder	93.2	90.4	94.4	89.5	86.4	78.9	86.1	75.0	77.7	75.0	81.9	63.0
Rape	100.0	81.0	72.4	70.6	76.3	76.2	51.7	41.2	63.2	57.1	48.3	35.3
Robbery	89.1	92.3	84.2	82.1	75.5	72.1	66.5	62.5	64.1	59.7	53.1	47.8
Burglary	85.3	85.2	76.2	82.3	67.4	65.4	57.6	63.6	57.1	56.2	48.9	54.4
Larceny	88.1	90.7	85.2	88.1	75.7	79.0	66.4	66.6	64.5	71.6	59.2	54.7
MVT	84.1	83.0	79.0	77.5	61.9	64.2	61.8	53.9	47.6	52.8	51.3	42.2
Forgery	90.2	93.2	87.0	81.8	77.7	78.4	74.8	62.5	72.3	67.1	60.0	55.7
Drug	98.5	95.7	88.4	87.7	89.3	81.7	75.7	71.3	77.1	71.3	64.7	63.7
Assault	92.0	91.8	85.0	82.5	74.0	81.6	65.0	63.8	68.0	79.3	60.0	63.7
Traffic/DWI	88.9	90.9	88.8	83.8	72.2	85.5	73.8	76.3	63.9	78.2	66.3	71.3
Gender												
Male	89.2	88.7	82.7	83.7	74.2	73.4	66.0	65.1	64.2	63.8	56.8	55.5
Female	92.7	98.7	88.6	91.1	83.6	87.0	78.7	76.8	78.2	84.4	66.7	65.3
Age												
18–22	83.9	86.4	75.9	74.1	65.1	66.9	57.7	54.2	55.4	56.5	51.4	43.9
23–27	89.0	88.3	79.5	82.1	74.4	74.1	64.5	64.1	65.1	64.5	53.4	52.4
28–32	92.4	90.9	84.9	85.4	76.0	71.5	68.7	63.3	63.9	61.6	56.9	54.5
33–37	91.4	89.1	83.8	87.8	79.2	75.6	65.8	71.4	72.4	65.4	55.8	61.8
38–42	91.1	92.3	91.2	93.6	74.2	76.9	74.8	77.6	61.3	71.4	68.7	71.8
43+	88.2	90.8	89.8	90.9	80.9	85.5	74.9	78.9	73.7	79.4	69.5	69.7
Race/ethnicity												
Anglo	91.3	90.6	86.8	86.5	77.6	79.3	71.3	69.3	70.2	72.0	67.5	62.0
African-American	88.0	86.7	82.3	81.5	72.0	69.1	65.6	60.9	61.8	58.6	54.1	48.5
Latino	88.7	91.9	76.7	85.4	75.3	73.3	60.1	69.3	61.8	63.3	54.0	59.2
Assessed risk												
High	78.4	83.5	74.1	77.7	62.1	59.0	53.7	53.4	48.4	51.8	43.1	42.2
Medium	89.1	88.4	82.1	83.0	73.3	73.0	66.4	63.4	63.0	62.9	56.9	53.1
Low	94.7	94.5	92.4	91.4	83.6	84.6	78.1	79.4	77.0	76.8	69.7	71.9

five months following release, parolees in the 1986 cohort have somewhat lower survival probabilities. This trend continues until about the thirteenth month of release. Thereafter, parolees in the 1987 cohort have slightly lower survival probabilities.

Table 4.1 presents the cumulative percent surviving in each cohort at twelve, twenty-four, and thirty-six month intervals. After twelve months the proportion surviving among all parolees in the 1984 and 1985 cohorts were identical—89.5 and 89.4 percent respectively. Members of the 1986 and 1987 cohorts were less likely to survive to the end of the first year—83.1 percent and 84.4 percent respectively.

The survival rates after twenty-four months demonstrate a similar pattern. The 1984 and 1985 cohorts had survival rates that are again virtually identical—74.9 and 74.3 percent. Consistent with the pattern for the first twelve months of release, the 1986 and 1987 cohorts exhibit a lower survival rate. As a whole, approximately one-third of the parolees in the 1986 and 1987 cohorts were reincarcerated after twenty-four months, compared to approximately 25 percent for the 1984 and 1985 cohorts.

These trends continue during the third year of release. The percent surviving from the 1984 and 1985 cohorts is essentially identical (approximately one-third were returned to TDC by the end of the third year). The rates for the 1986 and 1987 cohorts are quite similar as well, although the failure rate is again considerably higher in these later cohorts (approximately 44 percent were returned after thirty-six months).

The differences across cohorts become clearer when we examine the six-month moving average of the monthly hazard rates in Figure 4.2. Moving averages were computed in order to obtain a clearer trend, undistorted by month-to-month fluctuation. The data indicate quite similar rates for the first two cohorts, with an increase in the first twelve months, a leveling off at the maximum rates for a period of a few months, a gradual decline, and then a second leveling off.

In comparison, the hazard rates for the 1986 cohort increased faster and peaked sooner than those for the others. There was then a decline and a second increase at about fifteen months, tracking the peak for the earlier cohorts. Thus, not only is the overall *level* of reincarceration higher for the 1986 cohort, this cohort also exhibits a distinctively different *pattern*. It is important to keep this distinction between level and pattern firmly in mind. Fluctuations in the pattern—what has been called the basic "transition curve"—seem to be most directly linked with administrative actions. Some shifts in the level of reincarceration appear to be more a function of a reduced deterrent effect. This will be explored in greater detail later in this chapter.

The hazard rate trends for the 1987 cohort are also different still from the other cohorts. In terms of its pattern, the 1987 group is more similar to the 1984 and 1985 cohorts in that these three cohorts have rates that

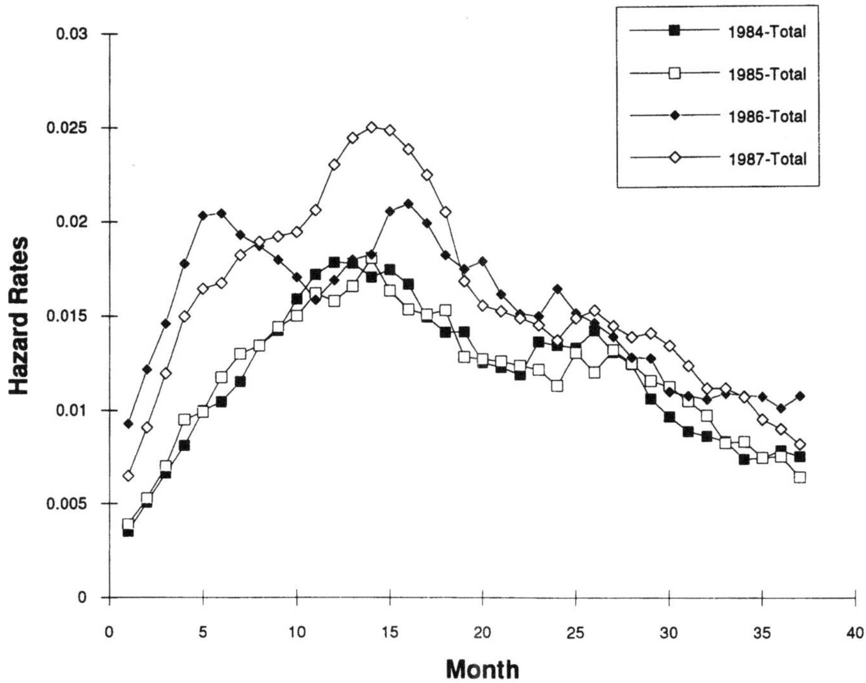

FIGURE 4.2. Hazard rates for the 1984–1987 cohorts. Reproduced with permission from Kelly and Ekland-Olson, "The Pesponse of the Criminal Justice System to Prison Overcrowding." *Law and Society Review*, Vol. 25, No. 3: 601–20, 1991. © Law & Society Association.

increase monotonically up to approximately the twelfth to fourteenth month and then gradually decline as the release period increases. What differentiates the 1987 cohort is the probability that persons would return to prison within a given time frame. The peak rates for the 1987 cohort, while occurring at approximately the same time as the other cohorts, are considerably higher than the 1984, 1985, or 1986 cohorts.

Thus, it appears that the survival probabilities and hazard rates for the 1984 and 1985 cohorts can serve as a baseline from which to evaluate the trends for 1986 and 1987. It is clear that the 1986 and 1987 cohorts departed from the baseline, but in different ways. The 1986 cohort differs in that there was an early peak in the hazard rates, followed by a decline, and then a second peak. The 1987 cohort is unique in the sense that while the pattern in hazard rates is parallel to the 1984 and 1985 rates, the overall level is considerably higher. These departures from the baseline years of 1984 and 1985 are the first bits of evidence that the changes occurring in the administration of criminal justice during these years did, indeed, result in shifts in both the pattern and level of reincarceration among those released on parole in the later years. We now turn to an evaluation of the probable reasons for these trends.

Correlates of Recidivism across Cohorts

We have taken as our central research problem the question of whether, in the context of large-scale, rapid change in the criminal justice system, there were changes in the patterns and probabilities that persons would end up back in prison after being released on parole. After comparing parolees released in 1984 and 1985 in chapter 3, the answer to this question is a clear no. In both years, the three-year patterns of return reflect the often-noted transition curve (e.g., Irwin 1970; Minor and Courlander 1979; Rossi et al. 1980; Ekland-Olson et al. 1983). These patterns are quite consistent with national data for the same time frame. In this sense, it can be said that the broad-based changes in the criminal justice system, precipitated by the federal court intervention in *Ruiz*, had little if any impact on recidivism among these parolees.

In contrast, persons released on parole in 1986 and 1987 had higher return rates. The 1986 cohort also departed from the basic transition curve with a bimodal distribution and an accelerated return pattern early in the release period.

We have noted several potential explanations for these patterns. Of these explanations, the administrative discretion and compositional change alternatives appear most relevant for the unique pattern of return in the 1986 cohort. On the other hand, an altered deterrent effect from the criminal sanctioning process and administrative discretion are most useful for understanding the 1987 pattern.

We first consider the extent to which the 1986 cohort differs compositionally from the prior cohorts and thus the extent to which such differences may account for its distinctive survival and hazard rate trends. Table 4.2 presents the percentage distributions for each cohort, broken down by prior incarceration offense, gender, age, ethnicity/race, and assessed risk. Given findings that region of the state to which persons were paroled made no discernable difference, it has been excluded as a variable in the following analyses.

While there are some relatively minor differences between the 1986 and earlier cohorts (e.g., a higher percentage of parolees with a prior incarceration offense of burglary), the most important compositional shift is the increase in 1986 in the proportion of high-risk parolees. The question becomes whether this increase in parolees assessed as high risk in the 1986 cohort accounts for the differential in the survival probabilities. The answer is a qualified yes.

It is quite likely that the increase in high-risk parolees contributes to the lower survival rates for the 1986 cohort (table 4.1). However, this

TABLE 4.2. Percentage distributions for the 1984–1987 cohorts.

	Cohorts			
	1984	1985	1986	1987
N	1,435	1,119	1,671	2,073
Release offense				
Murder	7.2	4.6	4.3	3.7
Rape	2.6	1.9	1.7	.8
Robbery	13.4	11.5	9.8	8.9
Burglary	29.9	30.2	32.9	27.6
Larceny	14.6	14.5	13.3	13.4
MVT	4.4	4.7	4.5	4.9
Forgery	7.8	7.9	6.9	8.5
Drug	9.1	10.3	11.8	17.7
Assault	3.5	4.4	3.6	3.9
Traffic/DWI	2.5	4.8	4.8	3.9
Gender				
Male	92.3	93.1	93.2	90.8
Female	7.7	6.9	6.8	9.2
Age				
18–23	13.0	13.8	13.2	14.6
24–27	32.3	30.0	29.1	26.9
28–32	20.1	23.5	23.3	24.3
33–37	15.4	13.9	14.4	16.6
38–42	8.6	8.1	8.8	7.6
43+	10.6	11.7	11.2	10.1
Ethnicity/race				
Anglo	41.7	42.7	40.7	41.7
African-American	39.0	38.4	40.2	37.6
Latino	19.2	18.8	18.7	20.1
Assessed risk				
High	10.7	12.4	16.4	12.1
Medium	61.7	61.4	61.5	62.8
Low	27.6	26.1	22.1	25.1

cannot be the entire explanation. If the lower survival probabilities and hazard rates for the 1986 cohort are solely due to compositional shifts, we would not expect to see differences *within* risk categories. That is, we would not expect to find, as indeed we do, that high-risk parolees in 1986 experienced substantially lower survival rates compared to their counterparts in 1985 and 1984.

It is, of course, possible that the observed patterns are due to compositional changes *within* risk categories. That is, it may be that high-risk parolees in 1986 and 1987 were higher risks compared to their counterparts in the earlier cohorts. To determine if this is a plausible explanation, we computed mean risk scores for each category of assessed risk for each cohort and found essentially no difference. Thus, we conclude that the trends in survival and hazard rates for 1986 are only in part a function of the increased proportion of high-risk parolees.

In the case of the 1987 cohort, the compositional explanation fails almost entirely. Table 4.2 indicates that on most dimensions, the 1987 cohort was quite similar to the 1985 cohort. Moreover, on the basis of the differential distribution of other characteristics in the 1987 cohort, one might hypothesize that the survival probabilities would, if anything, be lower for the 1987 cohort. Specifically, when compared to the 1985 cohort, the 1987 cohort had proportionally fewer parolees with incarceration offenses of burglary and larceny; had relatively more parolees with a prior incarceration offense involving drug trafficking; had relatively more females; was relatively older; and had proportionately fewer high-risk parolees.

Turning to the administrative discretion explanation, we note that during the time frame of this research the parole system found itself in a double bind. On the one hand, there was pressure to manage the crowding-induced crisis in the Texas prison system. This meant that prison beds and parole revocations had to be treated like precious resources. On the other hand, as noted earlier, increased media attention to the revolving prison door meant greater political pressure and public concern over the release of dangerous felons.

As discussed in chapter 2, publicity and political pressure surrounding the release of convicted felons reached a peak in 1986 and 1987. It was also during this period that the total number of persons released from TDC increased by approximately 40 percent (from 23,333 in 1985 to 33,370 in 1987). The resultant political and administrative pressures corresponded to the months of heightened hazard rates among members of the 1986 parole cohort. It is plausible, therefore, to hypothesize that the early peak in hazard rates for members of the 1986 cohort was reached when parole officers responded to the heightened public concern through the increased use of technical violations when there were indications that parolees were getting into trouble or committing new offenses.

There is some evidence to suggest that this was indeed the case. Among persons paroled in 1986, 20 percent of those revoked on technical grounds returned to prison within the first six months. The corresponding percentages for the 1984 and 1985 cohorts were 5 and 6 percent respectively or about one-quarter of the first six-month rate of the 1986 cohort.

As we also noted in chapter 2, violations of the technical conditions of parole return persons to prison more efficiently. They also fill the prison sooner. Hence, the double bind on the parole system. Legislation related to the prison crowding side of the double bind came in the form of Senate Bill 1167 which took effect just prior to the release of the persons included in our 1986 cohort. The explicit purpose of this legislation was to allow prison officials to reinstate good-time credits (after ninety days of satisfactory institutional adjustment) accumulated during the returning individual's previous stay in prison. This resulted in substantially shortened lengths of stay for those returned for technical reasons. Thus, for the person who had committed a new crime, a technical revocation rather than a new conviction was a better deal. Ironically, the legislative intent of reducing prison crowding resulted in aggravation of the revolving door of release and return.

In this regard, the patterns of technical violations reveal a selective discretion among parole officers. As political pressures increased to get high-profile criminals off the streets, the proportion of technical parole violations rose. When concerns with crowded cell blocks took over, and convicted felons began backing up in local jails, technical violations began to fall. This roller coaster pattern is evidenced by the finding that technical violations were more likely to be used early in the 1986 cohort, but over the total time period of the study they were less likely to be applied than in the 1985 cohort. By the time the 1987 cohort had been in the community for three years, the rate of technical violations had returned to levels characteristic of the 1984 cohort (about 8 percent of the total returned to prison).

To explore the extent to which the early use of technical violations in the 1986 cohort might explain the differences between reincarceration

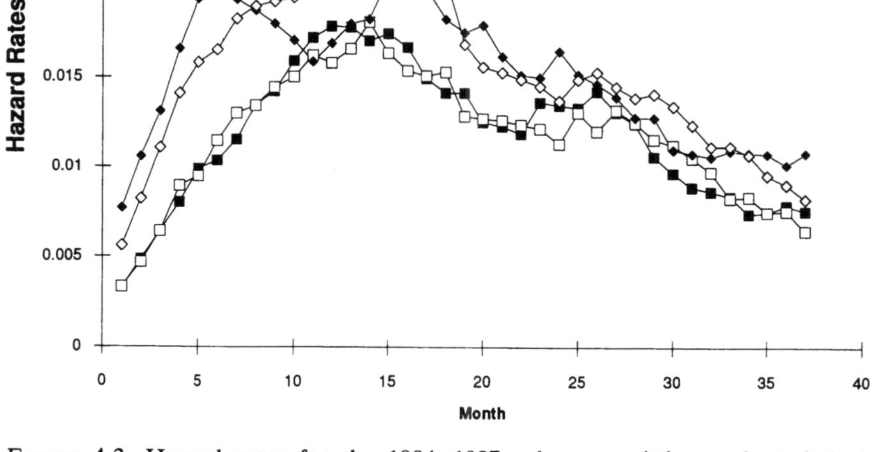

FIGURE 4.3. Hazard rates for the 1984–1987 cohorts, omitting early technical revocations.

rates across cohorts, we removed from each cohort those parolees who were returned to prison during the first six months of release for a technical violation and recomputed hazard-rate curves (figure 4.3). As is readily apparent, early technical revocations alone do not explain the noted differences across cohorts.

While the curves become somewhat more parallel, they do not begin to overlap. Technical revocations alone do not generally send persons back to prison, especially when the receiving prisons are already full. Rather, technical revocations are often used for more expeditious handling of high-profile cases where the person charged is suspected of committing another crime and where the parole offense is more serious than the new charge.

A technical revocation is the major tool parole officers have for controlling bad publicity from widely publicized cases. Evidence to support this basic point comes from data showing that in each of the release cohorts, for those who returned to prison, persons on parole for murder, sexual assault, and assault charges were the most likely to receive a technical revocation. For example, in the 1986 cohort, 40 percent of those on parole for a sentence of murder who returned to prison were returned on a technical revocation. The comparable percentage for those on parol for sexual assault and assault incarceration offenses was 30 percent. By contrast, only 13 percent of the recidivist burglars returned to prison following a technical revocation. This basic pattern held across cohorts.

As illustrated in table 4.2, the difference may be due to an overall higher rate of reincarceration among these individuals in the 1986 and 1987 cohorts. The most dramatic difference in characteristic-specific survival patterns across cohorts is evident among those released on parole after serving time for sexual assault. At the end of thirty-six months, in the 1986 and 1987 cohorts, only 48 and 35 percent of these parolees respectively were still in the community. This is the lowest three-year survival percentage of any category.

The question becomes whether this increased recidivism was due to a rise in criminal activity (possibly a reduced deterrent effect) or to heightened administrative sensitivity to these more high-profile offenders. The possibility of a reduced deterrent effect among this subcategory of parolees is made less likely, though not eliminated, by the finding that the percent returning for reconviction on repeat violent offense charges remained at a relatively constant 35 to 40 percent across the four cohorts, which would not indicate a reduced deterrent effect. This pattern of repetitious offending patterns is not the same across other types of offenses.

A contrasting pattern is found in the *overall* tendency between 1984 and 1987 for persons to be returned to prison for the same crime for which they were released. This is evidenced in table 4.3. When specific crime categories are compared, the percent of persons returning to prison for the same crime (e.g., released robbers returned for a robbery conviction) rose from 27.2 to 39.8 percent. Aggregated percentages of those who returned to prison for their release offense (e.g., released property offenders returned for another property offense) rose from 44.7 to 57.6 percent comparing the 1984 and 1987 cohorts.

This pattern of increased, repetitious offending is most evident among property offenders, and in particular in the chances that recidivist burglars would return to prison on a new burglary charge. Among persons returning to prison for repetitious burglary convictions, the percentage with new burglary or larceny/stolen property offenses rose from 39 percent to 49 percent between 1984 and 1986. This, then, is the first evidence we find indicating a possible reduction in the deterrent influence from an overburdened criminal justice system.

Given these findings, we decided to remove early returning (within the first nine months) technical violators as well as those on parole for sexual assault and burglary from each of the cohorts. In this way we hoped to assess the most obvious combined effects of administrative discretion, composition, and possibly reduced deterrence across cohorts. The resulting hazard rate curves for each cohort are presented in figure 4.4.

As is apparent, the variation across cohorts is thereby greatly reduced, though not totally eliminated. From this same figure we find that as

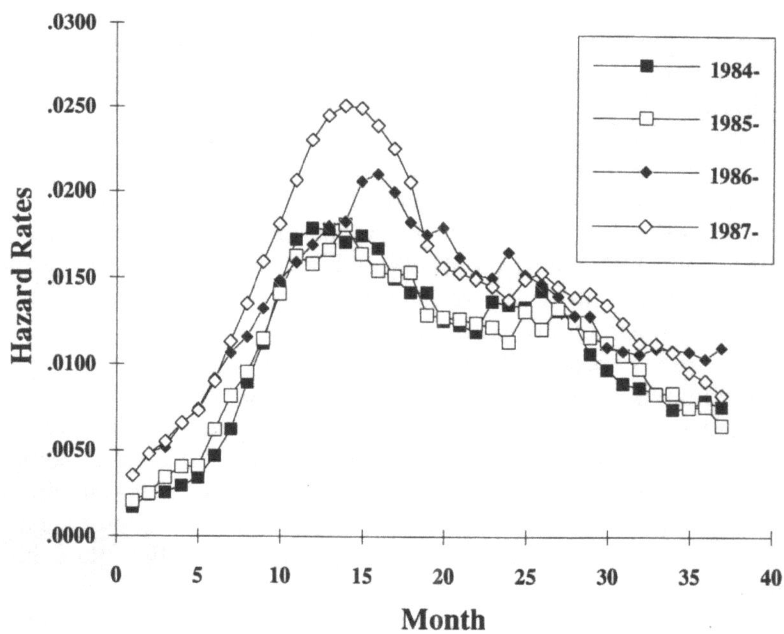

FIGURE 4.4. Hazard rates for the 1984–1987 cohorts, omitting parolees with technical violations, sexual assaults and burglary offenses who returned within the first nine months.

members of the 1985 cohort entered the middle of their second year of release, the months corresponding to the heightened return rates in the 1986 cohort, the probability of persons returning to prison began to rise. This further underscores the already noted administrative effect stemming from heightened public and political concern during these months. Thus, it appears that the differential timing of return to prison, characteristic of the 1986 cohort, was primarily a function of administrative discretion, cohort composition, and perhaps the reduced deterrent effect among property offenders.

We now turn to the reincarceration patterns for the 1987 cohort. We have already seen that compositional differences do not account for the heightened recidivism among these individuals. Moreover, there is little evidence to suggest that the administrative discretion explanation is as relevant as it was for the 1986 cohort. Figures 4.2 and 4.3 indicate that the pattern of return among those released in 1987 is essentially unaffected by the adjustments for early technical revocations, property offenses, and sexual assault incarceration offenses.

The strained resources explanation does not appear to be relevant for the 1987 patterns either. Data from the Texas Board of Pardons and Paroles, reported in chapter 2, indicate that parole officer case loads were

TABLE 4.3. Cross-tabulation of prior incarceration offense by return offense by release cohort.

Prior incarceration offense	Return offense		
	Violent	Property	Drug
1984			
Violent	35%	23%	9%
property	15	52	8
drug	23	20	30
1985			
Violent	36%	26%	7%
property	12	60	9
drug	22	24	46
1986			
Violent	40%	25%	5
property	13	59	14
drug	8	23	53
1987			
Violent	36%	33%	11%
property	10	70	10
drug	5	33	54

Reproduced with permission from Kelly and Ekland-Olson, "The Response of the Criminal Justice System to Prison Over-crowding." *Law & Society Review*, Vol. 25, No. 3: 601–20, 1991. © Law & Society Association.

in fact declining between 1986 and 1988. The ratio of parolees to officers was somewhat lower in 1988 (74:1) than in 1984 (81:1), 1985 (92:1), 1986 (93:1), and 1987 (90:1).

What we are left with, then, is the question of how changes in the criminal justice system during these years might have affected the estimates of the certainty and severity of punishment among offenders. While we do not have direct perceptual measures, and are thus unable to test the strict versions of the deterrence doctrine (Gibbs 1975), we do find selective increases across cohorts that persons released on parole would return to prison on charges close or identical to their earlier offense.

As is clear from table 4.3, this increase is most marked among property offenders. This, of course, is consistent with the idea that property offenses, more so than other crimes, are linked to the rational calculations implied by deterrence explanations. The same pattern is also found among persons released and then reconvicted on drug trafficking charges. In the 1984 cohort, 30 percent of those released after serving a sentence for a drug trafficking charge returned after a conviction for a similar offense. This return rate rose to 54 percent in 1987, an 80 percent increase.

Conclusion

During the 1980s, the administration of criminal justice in Texas, as in many other states, underwent dramatic restructuring primarily because of a burgeoning prison population and the resulting pressure from the federal courts. It was widely charged that this restructuring resulted in a seriously flawed criminal justice system. Those making sentencing decisions, so the argument went, were reacting to crowded prison conditions rather than to the nature of the offense. These conditions resulted in the process taking on the characteristics of a lottery in the sense that one's sentence was increasingly determined by the timing of the conviction rather than the conviction offense. Moreover, it was noted that due to variation in sentencing and release decisions over the years, dangerous and otherwise high-risk individuals were leaving and returning to prison through rapidly revolving prison doors.

The research we have reported was designed to examine these changes with data collected from four successive cohorts of parolees in Texas. There was some indication that the composition of these cohorts did change over the time period covered. More high-risk parolees were released, which should come as no surprise in light of the increasing reliance on parole release. There was also evidence that independent of compositional changes, recidivism rates rose in the 1986 and 1987 cohorts.

We first suspected that the dramatic increase in the hazard rates for the 1986 cohort was due primarily to high-risk offenders and those reincarcerated for technical violations. However, when these subgroups were omitted from the samples, the early spike still remained.

We then plotted the hazard rates for the specific prior incarceration offenses and discovered that the offense categories contributing the most to the curves were burglary (about one-third of the sample) and sexual assault (while there is only a small number they experienced very high early hazard rates). Other offense categories had hazard-rate trends consistent with the earlier overall patterns. When the cohorts were equated in terms of early returning burglary, sexual assault, high risk, and technical revocations, the survival curves and hazard rate *patterns* came closer together, but the 1986 and 1987 cohorts remained more likely to return to prison than those in the earlier years.

It is essentially impossible for parolees with new offenses to be processed through the system and to return to prison in five to six months if a trial is held. The early return scenario that makes the most sense is that these parolees, rather than being processed through the court system, elected to plead guilty to a technical violation. Why? First, the courts were crowded. Thus, prosecutors and judges were motivated to accept such a plea. Second, in 1985, the Texas legislature passed legislation giving parolees who returned to TDC on a technical violation the good time they had accumulated during their prior incarceration. Thus, parolees could plead guilty to a technical violation and begin their sentence with a dramatic head start on a future release.

The consequence of this law, designed to accelerate the release time of those with prior incarcerations, actually exacerbated the prison-crowding problem along with the administrative burden of prison officials by encouraging the quick return of offenders and by reducing the amount of time between admission and release. In addition, S.B. 1167 may very well have reduced the deterrent effect of reincarceration among a subgroup of parolees by reducing or minimizing the punishment associated with the commission of a new offense. Evidence for this possibility comes from heightened rates of repetitious criminal activity, especially among property and drug offenders.

What produced the decreased survival rates in the 1986 and 1987 cohorts? They appear to be the result of several coincidental factors, all of which are simultaneous responses to prison crowding that affect the pattern of reincarceration and the overall level of return. These factors include changes in the composition of the parole cohorts, public pressure that encouraged the early revocation of parole, and legislation that unintentionally increased the incentives for technical revocations and a possible reduction in deterrence. When combined, these factors produced the ironic result of increased reincarceration rates at a time of maximum pressure on the capacity of the Texas Department of Corrections.

One final point should be mentioned. During this period of dramatic renovation of the criminal justice system in Texas, there were no departures from the basic demographic correlates of involvement in crime. Cross-tabular analyses of parolee characteristics (not presented here) by outcome (reincarcerated versus not reincarcerated) produced significant chi square statistics ($p < .01$) for release offense, gender, age, race/ethnicity, and assessed risk. There were no discernable patterns of change in these relationships over time.

The results of the cross-tabular analyses indicate that assessed risk has the strongest bivariate association with the outcome variable. Age is the second strongest correlate in all cohorts. These findings are entirely consistent with other research conducted in settings where less dramatic changes in the administration of criminal justice were taking place. They are investigated in greater detail in the next chapter.

5 Multivariate Prediction of Reincarceration

As states continue to rely on parole as a means of easing prison crowding and as political pressure accumulates regarding associated public safety risks (for example, Austin 1986; Hoffman and Stone-Meierhoefer 1979; Petersilia and Turner 1986; Gottfredson and Tonry 1987, among others), prediction of who is more or less likely to recidivate becomes increasingly important, especially in light of the attention being given to selective incapacitation (Blumstein et al. 1983; Greenwood 1983; Greenwood and Abrahamse 1982; von Hirsch and Gottfredson 1983–84; and Klein and Caggiano 1986).

The purpose of this chapter is to estimate multivariate prediction models of reincarceration with special attention to how these models might have changed when the administration of justice was itself undergoing marked changes. These models involve the prediction of two different outcomes. One is whether individuals were reincarcerated or not. The second outcome focuses on those who returned to prison and examines the length of time from release to reincarceration (survival time). The analyses reported in chapters 3 and 4 clearly indicate that we should expect some variation in the probability and timing of failure across cohorts as well as across individual parolee characteristics. Thus, the analyses in this chapter focus not only on the role of parolee characteristics in the probability and timing of return to prison, but also on changes in those characteristics over time (i.e., across cohorts).

Analysis of Parole Outcome

Parole outcome is first considered as a dichotomy: Did the person return to prison or not? The assumptions underlying ordinary least squares (OLS) regression estimators are either clearly violated or suspect (see Kmenta 1971; Hanushek and Jackson 1977). While some researchers have opted for the simplicity of regression in estimating models with dichotomous dependent variables, we feel that the disadvantages associated with the violation of critical assumptions clearly outweigh the advantages. For this reason we rely on the alternative log-linear estimator.

Log-linear analysis (Goodman 1972a, 1972b; Feinberg 1977; Knoke and Burke 1980) is a multivariate technique appropriate for the analysis of categorical dependent variables. The basic goal of log-linear estimation is to generate a best-fitting model, a model of main effects and higher-order interactions that is only as complex as need be to adequately reproduce the observed outcomes. Simply put, this process involves specifying main and interaction effects that result in a parsimonious model that provides a reasonable fit with the observed subcells and marginals. The result is an estimate of the net effects of the various predictor variables on release outcome.

Since parole outcome is unambiguously the dependent variable, we use a logit specification. The logit model differs from the general log-linear model in that the logit specifies a dependent variable rather than treating all variables as "response variables" (see Knoke and Burke 1980). In this sense, logit models are similar to OLS regression models.

Data and Model Fitting

To simplify the interpretation of the logit models, we recoded some of the variables in the analysis. First of all, since the vast majority of the parolees in each cohort were male, we restricted the data to include only males. Prior incarceration offense (PIO) was collapsed into three categories: violent (consisting of murder, sexual assault, robbery, and assault), property (consisting of burglary, larceny/theft, fraud/forgery, and motor vehicle theft), and drug offenses. Age was divided into three categories—18 to 27, 28 to 37, and 38 and older. The coding of race/ethnicity and assessed risk were not altered. Given the relative unimportance of region of parole release as evidenced in chapters 3 and 4, we have omitted this variable from the analysis. Finally, the follow-up period for each of the four cohorts is established at thirty-six months.

Fitting the optimal logit model involves comparisons of various specifications to determine if more complex models produce significantly lower chi square statistics per degree of freedom. We first estimated the null or empty model. This served as a baseline for determining the significance of main effects and higher order interactions. If particular main effects and/or higher-order interactions had chi square statistics that were significantly lower compared to prior models, the more complex specification was considered superior.

We began by estimating the full main effects model and then eliminated one main effect at a time to see if the chi square changed significantly. We then added the full two-way model and again successively eliminated one term at a time. The model deemed appropriate or optimal for all four

TABLE 5.1. Chi square statistics, associated probabilities, and reduction in baseline Chi square for the optimal models.

Cohort	X^2	Reduction in baseline X^2
1984	43.4	63%
1985	54.1	47
1986	42.9	67
1987	31.9	78

cohorts contains all of the main effects (prior incarceration offense, age, race/ethnicity, and assessed risk) as well as the prior incarceration offense by risk and the age by race/ethnicity two-way interactions. Table 5.1 presents, for each cohort, the chi square statistics and the proportional reduction in the baseline chi square due to the optimal model.

As is evident, the significance of the chi square statistics varies by cohort, but in general the optimal model reasonably accounts for the baseline chi square. Specifically, this model accounts for 63 percent of the baseline chi square for the 1984 cohort, 47 percent for the 1985 cohort, 67 percent for the 1986 cohort, and 78 percent for the 1987 cohort.

Several parameter estimates are produced from a logit analysis, including log-linear coefficients, logit or log odds coefficients, and finally odds coefficients. The logit coefficients (log odds) are analogous to regression coefficients in an additive regression equation. This prediction equation has the following functional form:

$$Phi^{o} = B^{o} + B^{p} + B^{e} + B^{r} + B^{a} + B^{pr} + B^{ae} \tag{5.1}$$

Phi^{o} is the log of the conditional odds of returning to prison; B^{o} is the marginal effect of release outcome within each cohort; B^{p} is the main effect of prior incarceration offense; B^{e} is the main effect of race; B^{r} is the main effect of risk; B^{a} is the main effect of age; B^{pr} is the two-way interaction of prior incarceration offense and risk; and B^{ae} is the two-way interaction of age/race. The *Bs* (Betas) correspond to lambdas from the log-linear model, such that $B = 2 * lambda$.

The odds coefficients (antilogs of the logit coefficients) express the same relation but in a multiplicative rather than an additive form. The prediction equation based on the odds coefficients is as follows:

$$R^{o} = T^{o} * T^{p} * T^{e} * T^{r} * T^{a} * T^{pr} * T^{ae} \tag{5.2}$$

R^{o} is the odds of returning; T^{o} is the mean effect of outcome; T^{p}, T^{e}, T^{r} and T^{a} are the main effects of prior incarceration offense, race, risk and age; T^{pr} is the two-way effect of offense and risk; and T^{ae} is the two-way effect of age/race. Again, these coefficients are antilogs of the logit

TABLE 5.2. Logit and odds coefficients for the optimal model.

	1984		1985		1986		1987	
	Logit coefficients	Odds coefficients	Logit coefficients	Odds coefficients	Logit coefficients	Odds coefficients	Logit coefficients	Odds coefficients
Overall effect	−.5132	.5986	−.5114	.5997	−.4584	.6323	−.2696	.7637
Main effects								
Violent	.2542	1.2894	−.1596	.8525	−.0452	.9558	.2086	1.2320
Property	−.0152	.9849	−.0220	.9782	.2226	1.2493	−.1086	.8971
Drug	−.2390	.7874	.1816	1.1991	−.1774	.8374	−.1000	.9048
Race								
Anglo	−.2908	.7477	−.2924	.7465	−.2532	.7763	−.0958	.9086
African-American	.2052	1.2278	.2296	1.2581	.0804	1.0837	.3242	1.3829
Latino	.0856	1.0894	.0628	1.0648	.1728	1.1886	−.2284	.7958
Age								
18–27	.1400	1.1503	.2158	1.2409	.3016	1.3520	.4384	1.5502
28–37	.0176	1.0178	.1222	1.1300	.0768	1.0798	.1526	1.1649
38+	−.1576	.8542	−.3380	.7132	−.3784	.6850	−.5910	.5538
Risk								
High	1.1798	3.2537	.8222	2.2755	.3078	1.3604	.7586	2.1353
Medium	−.3470	.7068	−.1022	.9028	.1024	1.1078	.0298	1.0302
Low	−.8328	.4348	−.7200	.4868	−.4102	.6635	−.7884	.4546

Two-way effects								
Prior offense by risk								
Violent* high	.2624	1.3000	−.0740	.9287	−.0260	.9743	.1002	1.1054
Violent* medium	−.1404	.8690	.1388	1.1489	.2630	1.3008	−.0432	.9577
Violent* low	−.1220	.8851	−.0648	.9373	−.2370	.7890	−.0570	.9446
Property* high	−.8192	.4408	−.4306	.6501	.4152	1.5147	−.1788	.8363
Property* medium	.4428	1.5571	.1624	1.1763	−.1646	.8482	.0276	1.0280
Property* low	.3764	1.4570	.2682	1.3076	−.2506	.7783	.1512	1.1632
Drug* high	.5568	1.7451	.5046	1.6563	−.3892	.6776	.0786	1.0818
Drug* medium	−.3024	.7390	−.3012	.7399	−.0984	.9063	.0156	1.0157
Drug* low	−.2544	.7754	−.2034	.8160	.4876	1.6284	−.0942	.9101
Race by age								
Anglo* 18–27	−.0206	.9796	.0398	1.0406	−.2374	.7887	−.1940	.8237
Anglo* 28–37	.0304	1.0309	−.0058	.9942	.0386	1.0394	.1396	1.1498
Anglo* 38+	−.0098	.9902	−.0340	.9666	.1988	1.2199	.0544	1.0559
African-American* 18–27	.0268	.9736	.2126	1.2369	.1230	1.1309	.1752	1.1915
African-American* 28–37	−.1184	.8883	.0740	1.0768	−.0598	.9420	−.3054	.7368
African-American* 38+	.1452	1.1563	−.2866	.7508	−.0632	.9388	.1302	1.1391
Latino* 18–27	.0474	1.0485	−.2524	.7769	.1144	1.1212	.0188	1.0190
Latino* 28–37	.0880	1.0920	−.0682	.9341	.0121	1.0214	.1658	1.1803
Latino* 38+	−.1354	.8734	.3206	1.3780	−.1356	.8732	−.1846	.8314

coefficients and express the net odds of being in a particular category of an independent variable, compared to the other categories of the variable.

The interpretation of the logit coefficients is quite similar to that of standardized regression coefficients. A positive coefficient represents an increased net likelihood of return to prison and a negative logit coefficient indicates a reduced net likelihood of return. The odds coefficients (antilogs of the logit coefficients) have a somewhat different interpretation. They express the relative odds of return compared to the other categories of a variable. Odds coefficients equal or nearly equal to unity indicate no effect of that category on the probability of return, in comparison to the cohort mean. Coefficients greater than one indicate an increased likelihood of return and those less than one represent a lower likelihood of return. We will focus primarily on the odds coefficients in the discussion that follows.

Table 5.2 presents the data for each cohort. When a logit model contains both main effects and higher-order interactions, the coefficients for the higher-order interactions serve as adjustments to the main effects in a fashion similar to interaction effects in multiple regression models. Since this is the case, interaction coefficients often are difficult to directly interpret. Rather than spending much time interpreting the two-way interactions separately, we rely on the total effect coefficients for purposes of interpretation. That is, we constructed cross-tabulated tables for prior incarceration offense by risk and race/ethnicity by age and then added together the main effect and interaction coefficients for a particular subcell. We then used these composite or fitted odds coefficients for interpreting the effects of the independent variables in the analysis.

In table 5.2 we see, for example, that in 1984 the main effects for prior incarceration offense indicate that violent offenders have a net odds of returning that is 1.6 times that of drug offenders (1.3 compared to .79) and 1.3 times that of property offenders (1.3 compared to .98). It is also evident that minorities have a higher odds of reincarceration when compared to Anglos. African-American parolees were 64 percent more likely than whites to return, and Latinos have an odds 46 percent higher than that of Anglo parolees. The data indicate a consistent decline in the likelihood of reincarceration with age, confirming once again the consistent influence of age and maturation when it comes to criminal activity (Gottfredson and Hirschi 1990). Finally, the scales designed to assess the risk of reincarceration, net of other influences, also proved to be accurate, with parolees assessed as high risk having an odds of returning that is 4.6 times the odds of those assessed as medium risk and nearly 7.5 times those assessed as low-risk parolees at the time of release.

Reflecting the findings reported in chapter 4, the data from the 1985 cohort are quite similar to those from the 1984 cohort. An exception is a shift in the pattern of main effect odds coefficients for prior incarceration offense. In the 1985 cohort, drug offenders exhibited the greatest likelihood of returning to prison when compared to the other general categories. Drug offenders are 1.4 times more likely to return when compared to violent offenders and have a 22 percent higher likelihood when compared to property offenders. As before, since these coefficients do not represent the total effect of these variables, this discussion of the patterns of these main effects should be considered illustrative.

Comparing ethnic groups, African-American parolees again reveal the greatest chances of reincarceration, with an odds that is nearly 70 percent higher than that of Anglos and 1.2 times that of Latino parolees. The declining criminal tendencies with age are again evident, with a slight increase in the difference (from 1.3 to 1.7 times) over the 1984 cohort when the youngest parolees are compared with those in the oldest category. Finally, while the differences across the categories of assessed risk are lower than those for the 1984 cohort, the high-risk group still has an odds of returning that is 4.7 times that for low-risk parolees and 2.5 times that for those assessed as medium risk.

Again reflecting the analysis reported in chapter 4, in 1986 the overall odds of returning to prison are higher than in prior cohorts. The pattern of main effects for prior incarceration offense in the 1986 cohort vary somewhat. Specifically, in contrast to the two earlier cohorts, property offenders have an odds of return to prison that is 1.5 times that for drug offenders and 1.3 times that for violent offenders. The main effects for the 1986 cohort again indicate higher odds of reincarceration among African-Americans and Latinos. The differences across age categories continued to expand in that in the 1986 cohort the youngest group of parolees had a likelihood of returning that was almost twice the level of the oldest. Among those released in 1986, as in previous years, the scale devised to assess the overall risk of returning to prison, net of other effects, proved to be correct.

Finally, for the 1987 cohort, the overall effect of outcome reveals that the three-year odds of return to prison are considerably higher than in previous cohorts (odds coefficient of .76, compared to .63 for 1986 and .60 for both 1985 and 1984). The main effects for the 1987 cohort reveal that the probability of returning to prison across categories of prior incarceration offenses is highest for violent offenders. Taken as a whole, these parolees were 1.4 times more likely to return to prison than both property and drug offenders. African-American parolees again had a decidedly higher risk of return. Parolees assessed as high risk upon release in 1987 were 4.7 times more likely to return compared to low-risk parolees and twice as likely as those assessed to be medium risks.

Continuing the widening differential between younger and older parolees across the years of the study, parolees between the ages of eighteen and twenty-seven were almost three times more likely to return to prison than those in their late thirties or older. Thus, it would appear that much of the increase in the probability of returning to prison between 1984 and 1987 arose from changing levels of criminal activity among this youngest group of parolees. Not only are younger persons more likely to engage in crime and return to prison—a tendency documented in every study done on the topic—they are also apparently more susceptible to changes in the way criminal justice is administered.

Table 5.3 presents data regarding a slightly more complex combination of characteristics. The interpretation of the coefficients in the upper panel for each cohort is essentially the net effect of assessed risk and prior offense over and above the effect of age and race/ethnicity. The interpretation of the lower panel is just the opposite—the effect of ethnicity/race and age over and above or net of the effect of risk and prior offense. For a particular coefficient (e.g., 1.4 for high assessed risk property offenders), the interpretation is that the odds of return for someone in that category is higher (approximately 40 percent higher for these offenders) when compared to the cohort mean.

Moreover, the comparison of the odds coefficients across two categories allows the determination of the relative odds of returning to prison. Thus, if the odds coefficient in one category is 1.4 and in another the coefficient is .50 (e.g., low assessed risk, violent offenders), we can say that the individuals in the first category had a 2.8 times greater chance of returning to prison. This format for presenting the analyses is useful, since combining the main and two-way effects provides a way to summarize the effects of the variables so as to overcome the problems inherent in attempting to make sense of particular odds coefficients associated with the two-way interactions.

Looking at the figures in table 5.3, one is struck by the consistency of results across combinations of categories of assessed risk and age. The 1986 cohort is the only group for which these basic, well-documented correlates of returning to prison while on parole do not hold across the board. The most likely explanation for this departure from the influence of individual characteristics is the salience of political and administrative discretion during the 1986–87 time period documented in chapter 4.

Beyond this single exception, several specific patterns are worth noting. Looking first within categories of prior incarceration offenses in the 1984 cohort, it is clear that as assessed risk declines, so do the odds of return. Among violent offenders, the likelihood of return to prison is eleven times higher for parolees with high assessed risk compared to those with low risk and nearly seven times higher than for those with medium risk. Similarly, high-risk property offenders have a higher likelihood of return compared to the other risk categories. High-risk property offender parolees were about 30 percent more likely to return to prison than those assessed to be medium risk and 2.2 times more likely than low-risk property offenders. High-risk drug offenders were considerably more likely to be reincarcerated when compared to drug offenders with medium and low risk. Specifically, parolees released after serving time for

TABLE 5.3. Fitted odds coefficients for each cohort.

1984 Cohort				
		Assessed risk		
		High	Medium	Low
Prior offense	Violent	5.4543	.7920	.4963
	Property	1.4126	1.0839	.6240
	Drug	4.4709	.4113	.2655
		Age		
		18–27	28–37	38+
Ethnicity/race	Anglo	.8425	.7844	.6324
	African-American	1.3749	1.1100	1.2126
	Latino	1.3139	1.2107	.8127
1985 Cohort				
		Assessed risk		
		High	Medium	Low
Prior offense	Violent	1.8015	.8843	.3889
	Property	1.4472	1.0389	.6226
	Drug	4.5195	.8011	.4763
		Age		
		18–27	28–37	38+
Ethnicity/race	Anglo	.9209	.8777	.5146
	African-American	1.6810	1.7584	.6737
	Latino	1.2342	.9348	1.0464
1986 Cohort				
		Assessed risk		
		High	Medium	Low
Prior offense	Violent	1.2669	1.3774	.5004
	Property	2.5744	1.1740	.6452
	Drug	.7720	.8408	.9048
		Age		
		18–27	28–37	38+
Ethnicity/race	Anglo	.8278	.8713	.6487
	African-American	1.6570	1.1023	.6968
	Latino	1.8018	1.3110	.7109
1987 Cohort				
		Assessed risk		
		High	Medium	Low
Prior offense	Violent	2.9078	1.2156	.5290
	Property	1.6019	.9501	.4744
	Drug	2.0901	.9469	.3743
		Age		
		18–27	28–37	38+
Ethnicity/race	Anglo	1.1602	1.2170	.5313
	African-American	2.5544	1.1870	.8723
	Latino	1.2571	1.0942	.3664

a drug offense and assessed as high risk are nearly ten times more likely to return when compared to medium risk and almost fourteen times more likely than parolees judged to be at low risk of returning to prison.

These patterns by risk are, of course, as expected—the greater the assessed risk, the higher the odds of returning to prison. In this sense, the scale used by the Parole Board for assessing the risk of returning to prison worked. The apparently heightened effects within the 1984 cohort may in part reflect the higher likelihood of technical revocations in 1984, the cohort that experienced the greatest proportion of technical revocations among those returned to TDC within three years.

Again, within the 1984 cohort, the pattern across categories of prior offense differs by level of risk. Among high assessed risk parolees, those with violent offenses have the greatest odds of return (odds coefficient of 5.45) when compared to property and drug offenders. Within both the medium- and low-risk categories, property offenders have a greater likelihood of return in comparison with violent and drug offenders. In fact, among those judged to be at medium risk for returning to prison, property offenders are the only ones with a return odds higher than the odds for the cohort taken as a whole. Finally, all three offense categories have odds coefficients lower than unity, among those with low assessed risk.

Looking at the extremes provides an indication of how much variation exists in the odds of returning. Parolees in the 1984 cohort, released on parole after serving a sentence for a violent offense and assessed to be at high risk of returning to prison, have an odds coefficient of 5.45, or 445 percent higher than the cohort mean. On the other hand, low-risk drug offenders, again within the 1984 cohort, have an odds coefficient of .275. This translates into high-risk violent offenders having a likelihood of returning to prison that is twenty times that of the comparison group of low-risk drug offenders in this release cohort.

When characteristics across the two panels of data from the 1984 cohort are combined, violent, high-risk, young, African-American parolees exhibit the greatest likelihood of returning to prison. The expected likelihood of returning to prison for parolees with these combined characteristics is reflected in an odds coefficient of 4.51. Low-likelihood parolees include low assessed risk drug offenders who are in their late thirties or older and are Anglo. Among these parolees the odds coefficient is .10. Thus, parolees with the high-likelihood characteristics have an odds of returning to prison forty-five times the odds for those at the low end.

Turning to the 1985 cohort, characteristics associated with a high probability of returning to prison fit the profile of being African-American, high assessed risk drug offenders between twenty-eight and thirty-seven years old. The odds coefficient for returning to prison among parolees with this combined set of characteristics is 4.77, or 377 percent greater than the cohort mean. The characteristics associated with low likelihood of return include low risk/violent and older Anglos. The odds coefficient for this combined set of characteristics is .12, or about one-tenth of the cohort mean. Comparing the high and low subgroupings reveals that the odds for the high group were approximately forty times higher than the odds for the low group.

For 1986, parolees with the characteristics of high assessed risk and property offenses who are also young and Latino have an odds coefficient for reincarceration of 2.9. Conversely, low assessed risk/violent offenders and older/Anglo parolees have an odds coefficient of .20. These results indicate that the high-probability group is just under fifteen times more likely to return to prison when compared to the low odds group for 1986.

Finally, the 1987 cohort high-probability subgroup consists of high assessed risk/violent prior offense and young/African-American. For this combined set of characteristics, the odds coefficient is 5.18. At the other end, the low-probability subgroup consists of older Latinos with low assessed risk scores and a prior drug offense. The odds coefficient associated with these characteristics is .25. Thus, the high probability group is over 20 times more likely to return compared to the low odds group in the 1987 cohort.

The most consistent findings across cohorts and combinations of characteristics are those for assessed risk and age. In every instance, high assessed risk is associated with the highest odds of return; low assessed risk is associated with the lowest probability of return. Young age at parole is associated with the highest likelihood of return, and older age at time of parole is associated with a lower probability.

On the other hand, among those with high assessed risk, there is considerable variation across cohorts with regard to which offense categories have the greatest probability of return. High-risk violent offenders were most likely to return in 1984, high-risk drug offenders in 1985, high-risk property offenders in 1986, and high-risk violent offenders in 1987. We would argue that this variation across crime type is largely due to shifting political and, hence, parole supervision priorities.

Much research has documented that property offenders return to prison more often when compared to violent offenders (e.g., Bureau of Justice Statistics 1984, 1989b). Thus, on the basis of past research, we would expect that the subgroup with the greatest odds of return should be high-risk property offenders. However, two factors affect the level of return to prison—criminal activity on the part of the offender population and the actions of the criminal justice system, especially when it includes the revocation of parole. If the only factor influencing return is the criminal behavior of offenders, then we would expect to see high-risk property offenders having the greatest odds of reincarceration. However, there has been considerable media attention and resulting public and political pressure focused on the criminal justice system, specifically the

Board of Pardons and Paroles. This pressure has been directed toward minimizing the perceived public safety risks associated with high-profile offenders.

Thus, one plausible explanation for the higher odds of return among high-risk violent and drug offenders is that heightened public and political pressure may have resulted in increased supervision of these parolees during this time period. The data are consistent with the idea that as these high-profile offenders were released, the parole system was more sensitized to the potential political and public safety consequences of releasing such offenders and thus may have devoted more effort to their supervision, detection of technical violations, and thus revolation and reincarceration.

Analysis of Survival Time

The prediction of parole outcome is not limited simply to success or failure. The trends in the hazard rates discussed in chapter 4 indicate that there are important differences in the timing of reincarceration—across cohorts as well as across parolee characteristics. The 1986 release cohort exhibited a rapid increase in the early months of the first year, a sharp decline, and then another peak around the fifteenth and sixteenth months. The 1987 cohort had the highest hazard rates of any of the cohorts, with a peak in the rates at approximately the fourteenth month. Moreover, hazard rates varied by characteristics such as prior incarceration offense and assessed risk. The purpose of this section is to determine the extent to which the factors that predict success or failure while on parole also are related to the length of time between release and return.

The dependent variable in this analysis is the length of time from release on parole to return to prison. Since a substantial proportion of each of the samples (cohorts) did not return to prison during the thirty-six month follow-up period (i.e., is statistically censored), OLS regression is an inappropriate estimator. Simply applying OLS regression to the subset of individuals who actually failed during the three-year period, excluding the censored observations, leads to severe bias in the parameter estimates (Sorensen 1977; Tuma and Hannan 1978; Schmidt and Witte 1988). Maximum likelihood techniques have been developed and used for the analysis of events in which not all individuals in a sample experienced the event (see Allison 1984, for a discussion of maximum likelihood estimation for event history analysis).

Analysis of survival time with regard to recidivism has been gaining in popularity in recent years (e.g., Carr-Hill and Carr-Hill 1972; Stollmack and Harris 1974; Maltz and McCleary 1977; Sherman and Berk 1984; Schmidt and Witte 1988). Researchers have relied on a variety of survival model specifications to predict time from release to failure, including nonparametric (such as proportional hazards models) and parametric models (such as the exponential, lognormal, and LaGuerre distributions). Both the parametric and nonparametric models take into account censoring, and thus are superior to OLS regression. A recent evaluation of various parametric and nonparametric survival models led Schmidt and Witte (1988, 18) to conclude "we are firmly convinced, on the basis of our work, that parametric models fit recidivism data better and provide more accurate predictions than nonparametric models do."

The selection of a particular parametric model depends primarily on the distribution of the hazard rates. The lognormal model assumes a nonmonotonic hazard distribution, specifically one that initially increases and then declines (Allison 1984; Schmidt and Witte 1988). Since the hazard distributions in our data are most similar to the distribution for lognormal models, we rely on that specification for the analyses conducted here (see Schmidt and Witte, 1988, for a detailed discussion of lognormal models).

The variables used in this analysis include: length of time (months) from release to return to prison; age, collapsed into 18 to 27, 28 to 37, and 38 and over; assessed risk (high, medium, and low); prior incarceration offense (violent, property, drug, and other); race/ethnicity (Anglo, African-American and Latino); and gender. Parolees who did not fail during the thirty-six month observation period are considered statistically censored. Similar to dummy variable regression, each variable has a reference group. In the analyses that follow, the reference groups are: age thirty-eight-plus, low risk, "other" prior offense, female, and white.

Table 5.4 presents the estimated coefficients and their antilogs from the lognormal models for the four release cohorts. Also presented are the log likelihood values and the significance of the variables in the models. Since the coefficients are in the log of length of time, the antilogs have a more straightforward interpretation, i.e., the antilog of the coefficient represents the proportion of time from release to return compared to the reference group. For example, the coefficient for high risk for the 1984 cohort (.460) has the following interpretation: high-risk parolees survived only 46 percent of the length of time that low-risk parolees survived.

The results from the estimation of the lognormal regression for the 1984 cohort indicate that all of the variables except age have significant net effects (the log likelihood is −1247). As expected, high-risk parolees have a survival time that, all else being equal, is 46 percent of that of low-risk parolees. Those with medium assessed risk have a survival time that is about 70 percent of that for the reference group of low-risk parolees. Finally, the difference between the high- and medium-risk groups is statistically significant.

The effect of prior incarceration offense is also significant, but primarily because of the effect of drug offenders who have a much higher relative survival time compared to violent and property offenders. The significant

TABLE 5.4. Estimated effect parameters and antilogs from lognormal survival models.

	1984 Cohort		1985 Cohort		1986 Cohort		1987 Cohort	
Variable	Coefficient	Antilog	Coefficient	Antilog	Coefficient	Antilog	Coefficient	Antilog
Age								
18–27	−.14	.86	−.35	.70	−.50	.61	−.59	.55
28–37	−.00	.99	−.35	.70	−.35	.70	−.42	.66
38+								
Risk*								
High	−.77	.46	−.77	.46	−.82	.44	−.82	.44
Medium	−.36	.69	−.39	.67	−.37	.69	−.51	.60
Low								
Offense*								
Violent	−.01	.98	−.09	.91	−.20	.81	−.24	.78
Property	−.15	.85	−.22	.80	−.27	.75	−.12	.88
Drug	.35	1.42	−.02	.97	−.12	.88	−.08	.92
Other								
Gender*								
Male	−.28	.75	−.75	.47	−.26	.77	−.36	.69
Female								
Race/ethnicity*								
African American	−.23	.79	−.38	.68	−.18	.83	−.26	.76
Latino	−.23	.79	−.17	.84	−.30	.73	.04	1.04
Anglo								
Intercept	4.88	132.0	5.71	303.2	5.12	167.5	5.16	175.6
Log likelihood		−1247		−973.2		−1706		−2077

* Variable has statistically significant effect at .01 level.

effects for this variable are limited to the comparison of violent and drug, and property and drug.

As expected, gender is an important predictor of survival time. On average, males survive approximately 75 percent of the length of time female parolees survive.

Finally, the effects of race/ethnicity confirm our earlier findings that white parolees survive longer than minorities. Both African-American and Latino parolees released in 1984 had survival times that were approximately 80 percent of the survival time experienced by Anglos. These results indicate that for this cohort, African-American and Latino parolees had essentially the same expected survival times, net of the other variables in the model.

The model for the 1985 release cohort is significant (log likelihood is −973); however, the pattern of effects is somewhat different from the previous model. The effects of age are significant; parolees between the ages of 18 to 27 and 28 to 37 return more quickly compared to those age 38 and over. However, there are no differences between the 18 to 27 and 28 to 32 age groups.

Again, assessed risk has a strong effect on return time. Parolees with high assessed risk experienced a survival time that is only 46 percent of that for those with low risk. The comparable proportion for medium-risk releasees is 67 percent. Again, the difference between high and medium risk is also significant.

Gender differences in return time are quite strong. Males have a survival time that averages about 47 percent of that for female parolees. The gender effect in this model is considerably stronger than that reported for the previous cohort. Finally, race/ethnicity has a significant effect on survival time. The effect is limited however to the difference between Anglo and African-American parolees, i.e., African-Americans and Latinos and Latinos and Anglos are not statistically different.

The variables that were significant predictors for the 1985 cohort are significant for the model estimated for 1986 releasees as well (log likelihood of −1707). The parameter estimates for age indicate that parolees eighteen to twenty-seven have a significantly lower expected survival time compared to the oldest age group. That pattern also holds for the twenty-eight to thirty-seven year age group. Finally, the 18 to 27 and 28 to 37 age groups are significantly different as well.

Once again, the effects of risk are the strongest. Those with high assessed risk have a net survival time that is 44 percent of that for parolees with low assessed risk. The group with medium assessed risk also differs significantly from the reference category of low risk. Moreover, those with high risk are significantly different from those with medium risk.

Gender continues to be an important predictor of survival time. Males have an average survival time that is 77 percent of that for females, net of the other effects in the model. While this is an important effect, it is considerably smaller than that reported for the 1985 cohort.

Latino parolees have an expected length of time from release to reincarceration that is just under 75 percent of that for the reference group of whites. African-American parolees also differ significantly from Anglos. However, the difference between African-American and Latinos is statistically trivial.

With one exception, the pattern of effects for the 1987 cohort are identical to that for the 1986 model. Overall, the 1987 model is significant with a log likelihood of −2077. The age effect is relatively quite strong. All of the age effects are significant, i.e., the 18 to 27 age group is different from the 38 plus age group, the 28 to 37 age group is different from the 38 plus group, and the two younger age groups are statistically different from each other. As expected, the youngest age category exhibits the greatest reduction in survival time (55 percent of that for parolees thirty-eight years and older).

High-risk parolees have a net survival time that is only 44 percent of that for those with low assessed risk. Those with medium risk have a time from release to reincarceration that is 60 percent of the low-risk group. Finally, high- and medium-risk parolees are statistically different as well.

The gender effect is important for this cohort. Males have a significantly lower average survival time compared to females (69 percent). With regard to race/ethnicity, African-American parolees have significantly lower survival times compared to Latinos and Anglos. However, Latinos and Anglos are essentially the same with regard to length of time from release to return. As has been the case with three out of the four cohorts, prior incarceration offense has a trivial effect on return time, net of the other variables in the model.

Across the cohorts, the effects of assessed risk are the strongest and the most consistent. We also observed consistently significant influences of gender and race/ethnicity. With regard to race/ethnicity, the one persistent difference is that between Anglos and other ethnic categories. In only one case were the differences between Latino and African-American parolees statistically significant. When significant, the effects of age were rather strong, indicating that not only do younger parolees have a greater likelihood of failure but also a shorter survival time after release. The one finding that is contrary to the results from prior descriptive analyses and the log-linear models estimated earlier in this chapter is the trivial net effect of prior incarceration offense. One likely explanation for this result is that other characteristics such as age and risk are associated with prior offense and once these factors are partialled out, offense has no effect.

A useful way to summarize the differences across the four models is to compute predicted values for survival time. Taking a worst case scenario, we base these predictions on the characteristics in each model that are statistically significant but that are also associated with the lowest survival times. The prediction equations for the four cohorts consist of the following characteristics:

1984—high risk, property incarceration offense, male, African-American
1985—18–27, high risk, male, African-American
1986—18–27, high risk, male, Latino
1987—18–27, high risk, male, African-American

These predicted values are obtained by multiplying the intercepts by the antilogs of the coefficients associated with the selected characteristics. The following equations were used to generate the predicted values:

1984 $S = 132 * .46 * .85 * .75 * .79$
$= 30.8$ *months*
1985 $S = 303 * .70 * .46 * .47 * .68$
$= 31.8$ *months*
1986 $S = 167 * .61 * .44 * .77 * .73$
$= 25.1$ *months*
1987 $S = 175 * .55 * .44 * .69 * .77$
$= 22.6$ *months*

S represents the predicted survival time in months; 132, 303, 167, and 175 are the intercepts; and the coefficients are the antilogs of the parameter estimates associated with the characteristics listed above.

Overall, assessed risk has the strongest impact on survival time. This conclusion is based on a comparison of the size of the coefficient for high risk and the difference between the coefficients for high and medium risk. These differences are the largest of all of the variables in the model.

A useful way to illustrate the impact of risk is to generate predicted survival times by substituting the coefficient for medium risk for the coefficient for high risk, leaving all of the other coefficients unchanged. The difference in predicted values illustrates the impact of high risk on expected survival times. The following equations were used to generate these revised predicted values.

1984 $S = 132 * .69 * .85 * .75 * .79$
$= 45.8$
1985 $S = 303 * .70 * .67 * .47 * .68$
$= 45.4$
1986 $S = 167 * .61 * .69 * .77 * .73$
$= 39$
1987 $S = 175 * .55 * .60 * .69 * .76$
$= 30.3$

Changing from high risk to the modal category of medium risk has a substantial impact on survival time. This change produces the following excess number of predicted survival months: 15, 13.6, 13.9, and 7.7 months for the 1984, 1985, 1986, and 1987 cohorts respectively.

Conclusion

The pattern of predicted values is quite consistent with our preliminary conclusions regarding trends in survival probabilities, hazard rates, and parole outcome in this and previous chapters. The early cohorts (1984 and 1985) have very similar predicted survival times. On the other hand, the 1986 cohort has an estimated survival time five months shorter than the prior two, and the 1987 cohort has a predicted time that is between eight and nine months shorter. What this suggests is that the factors in each cohort that maximize the level and swiftness of return to prison changed over time. We have suggested in chapter 4 that this is in part compositional, but also partly due to administrative changes (increased reliance on technical revocations), as well policy/legislative changes that may have lessened the deterrent effect of incarceration. While this analysis does not permit us to assess which of these factors is most important, it is clear that compositional differences play an important role as is evidenced by the substitution of the coefficient for medium risk for the coefficient for high risk.

The primary focus of this chapter has been the identification of factors related to the probability and the timing of parole failure. The substantive concern is the extent to which the results from multivariate prediction models are consistent with the descriptive results reported in chapter 4. We have found that the factors thought to predict parole outcome based on our earlier descriptive results also are related to success/failure when considered collectively in multivariate prediction models. Similar factors are also related to the timing of parole failure and are consistent with the results from descriptive analyses reported earlier. These results provide further and more rigorous confirmation of our earlier conclusions regarding the salience of factors such as assessed risk, age, gender, prior incarceration offense, and race/ethnicity for predicting outcome as well as the differentials in the timing of parole failure.

The prediction of the likelihood of return is useful in that it allows policymakers to assess the relative net importance of various parolee characteristics and thus better allocate resources to those parolees most likely to return to prison. Moreover, these types of models allow one to summarize simultaneously the differential probabilities of return for combinations of characteristics. The analysis of hazard distributions and survival time also provides important information with regard to the pattern of return, permitting the identification of parolee characteristics that are related to faster or slower return rates. Knowledge of those factors may also focus more attention on those less likely to reach the transition curve.

6
An Evaluation of the Legislative Response: The Prison Management Act*

As crimes, arrests, convictions, and incarcerations increased throughout Texas in the 1980s, the state found it increasingly difficult to comply with the *Ruiz* decision and, in particular, the mandate to limit the inmate population. Under the threat of "astronomical fines" of some $800,500 per day or $24 million per month, the Seventieth Legislature responded in part by passing a revised Prison Management Act in 1987. The primary objective of the new PMA was to speed up the release of eligible parolees by awarding administrative good-conduct time to those eligible for parole or by accelerating the parole eligibility and review date of selected inmates.

This chapter examines the consequences of the 1987 PMA, particularly the unintended consequences. As a politically crafted response to a difficult and complex policy dilemma, implementation of the PMA had, predictably, quite mixed results. The act did successfully relieve the prison system of short-term overcrowding and contributed to the state's avoidance of massive fines for contempt of *Ruiz* court orders. However, it also exacerbated the crowding problem in the longer term by speeding the release of the most recidivism-prone segment of the prison population. In addition to this phenomenon, which is the particular focus of this chapter, there were unforeseen legal and political ramifications as well.

Background of the Prison Management Act

The original enactment of the Texas PMA occurred in 1983, while the state was still litigating the *Ruiz* decision. In May of 1982, the system had been forced to close its doors to new admissions to avoid violation of population caps set by Judge Justice (Martin and Ekland-Olson 1987, 214–16). The response of Texas counties—particularly Harris County, which forced the issue by bringing inmates to the TDC in defiance of the

---

* This chapter was coauthored with Carl Reynolds.

closed-door policy—foreshadowed problems later in the decade that led to further reforms focusing on the front end of the system.

This temporary closing also prompted Governor Clements to create the Blue Ribbon Commission for the Comprehensive Review of the Criminal Justice Corrections System. The commission's report recommended enactment of several changes to alleviate overcrowding, but not a PMA per se. Instead, the proposal for a reformulated plan for prison management came from the prison system leadership. It was suggested in the context of similar legislation implemented or under consideration in a number of other states (e.g., Georgia, Florida, South Carolina, Michigan, Illinois, and Tennessee). The original statute defined the capacity of the prison system and created a triggering mechanism when the inmate population reached 95 percent of capacity.[1] At that point, eligible inmates would receive thirty days administrative good-conduct time, and could subsequently receive more good time or advancement of their parole eligibility dates if the overcrowding situation persisted.

The statute was not used until after the 1987 amendments, which are the particular focus of this chapter. It is interesting to note, however, that there was a special session amendment to the PMA in 1986, which, like its 1987 and 1991 descendants, had a particular political agenda.[2] The changes at that point seemed designed to decrease the likelihood that the early release procedure would be implemented, by requiring that the 95 percent triggering situation persist for at least five consecutive days or for twenty out of thirty days. This amendment accordingly decreased the likelihood that the governor would be confronted with the politically distasteful task of certifying an emergency overcrowding situation and presiding over early releases during the 1986 election cycle.

The Seventieth Legislature began regular session in January of 1987, just days after being cited for contempt by Judge Justice and faced with the prospect of daily fines for failure to remedy violations of court orders by April 1 of that year. Acting unusually quickly for the beginning of the session, the legislature responded by putting S.B. 215 into effect by February 20, 1987. In addition to the emergency release mechanism—the PMA amendments—S.B. 215 expanded probation diversion program authority, appropriated $12.6 million to the prison system to remedy shortcomings (primarily medical staffing), and appropriated $7.8 million to the Board of Pardons and Paroles to expand its "relief valve" capacity in the form of additional halfway house beds and intensive supervision programs. On March 13, the threatened fines were suspended based on the state's good faith response and, after the hearing on compliance, the fines were vacated.

---

[1] Art. 6184o, V.A.C.S.; Acts 1983, 68th Leg., p. 979, ch. 233 § 1.

[2] Acts 1986, 69th Leg., 3rd. C.S., ch. 8 § 2.

At the time of the contempt finding, overcrowding had begun to strain the classification-for-housing system and otherwise separated inmates began to mix in the cell blocks, dorms, dayrooms, and dining halls. Contrary to sound correctional policy, this mixing became another reason for the contempt finding. The premise of the PMA was that the parole-eligible pool of inmates within the larger inmate population was diminished and that parole decisionmakers were "scraping the bottom of the barrel" to effect sufficient releases to keep the system open. Enforcement of the revised PMA would expand the parole-eligible pool temporarily, providing enough inmates so that more palatable releases could be made, with particular attention to the unusual mixing problem.

The debate surrounding passage of S.B. 215 was characterized by an overwhelming emphasis on cutting the political liability of the early release program. The earlier versions of the statute had some limitations on inmates eligible for good time or parole advancement: the inmate had to be a trusty or a Class I (i.e., low security risk) inmate and could not be serving time under the law that singled out certain aggravated offenses and defendants with convictions involving the use or exhibition of a deadly weapon.[3]

As S.B. 215 made its way through the legislative process, it accumulated an ever-lengthening laundry list (detailed below) of restrictions on eligibility as legislators tried to avoid politically sensitive offenses until a new section of the statute was required simply for enumeration. This was particularly important because the bill was an emergency measure backed by the state's leadership and was expected to pass by a large voting margin in each house. It did, achieving the constitutional two-thirds majority needed for immediate effect: 25 ayes, 3 nays in the senate, and 129 ayes, 11 nays in the house.

As introduced, the bill defined one pool of inmates for the initial award of good time: those with offenses under section 30.02 of chapters 31, 32, and 33 of the penal code (property offenses), excluding first degree burglary. A second pool of inmates was defined for subsequent actions under the act if the initial triggering of good time did not resolve the overcrowding situation. The definition of this pool was similar to that which ultimately passed, except that it excluded inmates held in administrative segregation within thirty days of their potential release.

As the bill passed the senate, the "two-pool" idea was abandoned, to be replaced by one class of eligible inmates for all purposes, with the list of excluded offenses in place. Amendments in the house added new offenses to the list, including indecency with a child, solicitation of a

---

[3] Art. 6184o, now codified as Government Code, sec. 498.021 et seq., citing Art. 42.12, Sec. 3g, Code of Criminal Procedure. See also, Art. 42.18, Sec. 8(a), Code of Criminal Procedure.

child, arson, and the conspiracy, solicitation, or attempted offenses that would apply to any of the enumerated underlying crimes. Amendments during the process also placed additional mandates for the parole release and supervision of PMA releasees, such as victim restitution and drug testing.

Ironically, given the care taken by politically sensitive incumbents, there was one electoral result that can be tied at least in part to a legislators's vote on S.B. 215. The number of this bill became well-known in Texas among political consultants because of its association with an award-winning political advertisement by the Epstein Group on behalf of Senator Bill Ratliff, the successful challenger in 1988 to Senator Richard Anderson of senate district 1. The advertisement cited Anderson's vote for S.B. 215 with a shot of a burglar breaking into a house decorated for the holidays and featured a voice-over giving the incumbent credit for the fact that the felon would be "back home in time for Christmas." Although the incumbent had other liabilities, it is accepted political wisdom that the advertisement, much like the Willie Horton ads in the 1988 presidential campaign, played a significant role in Anderson's defeat.

Other unforeseen results attended the inclusion of the list of ineligible offenses. Jimmy Michael Rutledge, a convicted felon, convinced the Court of Criminal Appeals that by altering the eligibility for good time under the PMA and by applying that change to exclude him from the PMA's benefit he was detrimentally affected in violation of the *ex post facto* doctrine by an enactment subsequent to the commission of his offense.[4] The case and its progeny created a new class of inmates—the *Rutledge* class—whose offenses were committed after the original enactment of the PMA in 1983 but prior to the effective date, February 20, 1987, of the new PMA. These inmates are entitled to thirty days of good time, the amount provided for under the earlier versions of the PMA, whenever the PMA is triggered by overcrowding. The legislature's attempt to restrict application of the act was thus only partly successful, since "interim" inmates with the enumerated offenses still receive a sizable credit of good time toward their parole eligibility if the PMA is triggered.

The legislative history of the PMA has not yet ended. During the Second Called Session of 1991, the legislature enacted further amendments to the PMA as a small part of a comprehensive bill aimed at relieving the systemic backlog of convicted felons awaiting transfer to prison in jails around the state. H.B. 93 changed the PMA with yet another political twist, completely removing the governor from responsibility under the statute and replacing her with the executive director and board of the

---

[4] *Ex parte Rutledge*, S.W. 2d (Ct. Crim. App., 1987); see also, *Ex parte McQueen* S.W. 2d (Ct. Crim. App., 1988), *Ex parte Hinson*, S.W. 2d (Ct. Crim. App., 1988), *Ex parte Hardin*, S.W. 2d (Ct. Crim. App., 1988), *Ex parte Ruiz*, S.W. 2d (Ct. Crim. App., 1988).

consolidated Department of Criminal Justice.[5] The revised 1991 PMA also includes authority and procedures for using the release mechanism to address the county jail backlog.

Operation of the Prison Management Act

The 1987 version of the PMA defined the capacity of the TDC and declared that when the prison population reached or exceeded 95 percent of capacity, an overcrowding emergency existed and the state was not in compliance with *Ruiz*. When such a situation developed, the governor was to order the director of the TDC to award thirty days of administrative good time to all eligible inmates. If this was not sufficient to bring the prison population under 95 percent of capacity, the governor was to request that the prison director award additional time, not to exceed ninety days, and request that the Board of Pardons and Paroles advance by an equal number of days the parole eligibility and parole review date of eligible inmates.

Inmates were eligible for "emergency" good time or the acceleration of parole eligibility if they met the following conditions:

1. If they were serving a sentence of ten years or fewer.
2. If they did not have a history of and had not shown a pattern of violent or assaultive behavior either in the TDC or prior to incarceration.
3. If release would not increase the likelihood of harm to the public.
4. If they were not serving a sentence for a felony crime involving use or exhibition of a firearm.
5. If they were not incarcerated for one of the following offenses: murder; capital murder; voluntary manslaughter; kidnapping; aggravated kidnapping; indecency with a child; sexual assault; aggravated sexual assault; deadly assault on a law enforcement official; injury to a child or the elderly; incest; arson; robbery; aggravated robbery; sale or purchase of a child; first degree felony burglary; aggravated promotion of prostitution; compelling prostitution; sale, distribution, or display of material harmful to a minor; sexual performance by a child; possession of a deadly weapon in prison; the criminal attempt, conspiracy, and/or solicitation of any of the offenses listed above; aggravated manufacture or delivery of a controlled substance; and aggravated possession of a controlled substance, including marijuana.

Thus, in their attempt to balance the demands of public safety and prison crowding, legislators through S.B. 215 defined a group of exceptions,

[5] Acts 1991, 72d Leg., 2nd C.S., ch. ____, § 17

offenses that the legislature likely perceived the public would not approve of for early release. In large measure the excluded offenses involved violence, sexual offenses, drugs, and crimes against children. This left an estimated 40 to 45 percent of the prison population eligible for early release under the PMA—some 16,000 inmates at the time S.B. 215 was passed. Approximately 70 percent of these inmates had been sentenced for burglary, theft, or forgery.

In this way, legislation designed to ease prison crowding took on a touch of irony. The intent was to speed up the parole process in order to reduce the size of the prison population. However, as we have seen in earlier chapters and as others have found (e.g., Bureau of Justice Statistics 1989b), inmates *ineligible* for PMA release, composed mainly of offenders convicted of violent crimes, tend to have *lower* return rates than the PMA eligibles, which are largely property offenders. By including a large proportion of property offenders in the pool of inmates eligible for early release or accelerated parole review, the legislature may have provided additional oil for the revolving prison door.

The purpose of this chapter is to see if this was indeed the case. The Texas Prison System was closed under the provisions of the PMA on the following dates in 1987:

February	Closed	5th–9th 12th–16th 19th–23rd 26th–28th
March	Closed	1st–2nd 5th–9th 19th–23rd 26th–30th
April	Closed	2nd–6th 9th–12th
July	Closed	4th–6th 11th–13th 16th 24th–28th 31st
August	Closed	1st–3rd 6th–12th 18th–26th 28th–31st

Thus, the prison system came under the provisions of the PMA on twenty separate occasions in that year. At first glance, one might conclude that the PMA was successful in that much needed prison space was made available (see, for example, Austin 1986, for assessments of the impact of emergency early release programs on prison crowding). However, this may have been only a short-term success. Our focus is on the longer term. If in fact the PMA provided for the early release of inmates who, all else being equal, had a higher likelihood of returning to prison, then its effectiveness would remain an open issue.

To assess the overall success of the PMA, we conducted a survival analysis comparing a cohort of inmates released under the PMA with a comparable general release cohort consisting of inmates who did not receive accelerated release under the provisions of the PMA. The primary aim was to determine the extent to which PMA releasees differed from non-PMA releasees in terms of both the level and timing of parole failure.

Data and Methods

The PMA resulted in the first early release of parolees in March of 1987. Our PMA cohort consists of everyone who was released under the provisions of the PMA in that month. In order to assess the impact of accelerated release, it is necessary to obtain baseline survival and hazard rates for a control group. The baseline cohort is the 1987 release cohort discussed in chapter 5. We rely on the 1987 general release cohort for this comparison since it consists of inmates released in February of 1987. It is desirable for this comparative analysis to have a cohort that is proximate in time to the PMA cohort in order to minimize changes that may have occurred over time in the criminal justice system.

The variables in this analysis include parole outcome (reincarcerated versus not reincarcerated); length of time from release to return; age; race/ethnicity; gender; prior incarceration offense; assessed risk; and return offense. A total of 1,337 parolees are in the PMA cohort. As discussed in chapter 5, the general release cohort consists of 2,063 parolees. The follow-up period for both of these cohorts is thirty-six months.

The analysis in this chapter is similar to that conducted in prior chapters. We compute trends in survival probabilities and hazard rates to assess differences between the PMA cohort and the "normal" 1987 release cohort. We then focus on the plausibility of three explanations for any observed differences in survival and hazard rates: compositional differences between the PMA cohort and the baseline 1987 cohort; administrative discretion with regard to the use of technical revocations; and a lessened deterrence associated with reduced imprisonment time.

It is clear, given the nature of the PMA, that there should be compositional differences between the PMA and non-PMA release cohorts. One predictable difference should be the larger proportion of property offenders in the PMA cohort. One might also expect increased vigilance on the part of parole officers with regard to the PMA releasees, because of legislative intent, public pressure, and an awareness of an increased probability of recidivism among the PMA releasees. Finally, the awarding of additional administrative good time may have further lessened the punishment of prison, thus reducing its deterrent effect.

Results

The left-hand panel of table 6.1 presents the cumulative proportion surviving at twelve, twenty-four, and thirty-six months for the total March PMA cohort by specific parolee characteristics. After the first year, 22 percent of the PMA releasees had been reincarcerated. After twenty-four months, 39 percent had been returned, and by the end of the third year, 48 percent were back in prison.

Parolees released after drug-trafficking convictions fared better on release compared to property offenders and those with "other" prior incarceration offenses. After thirty-six months, 61 percent of drug offenders and 49 and 50 percent respectively of persons released after serving time for property and other types of crimes survived on parole.

As expected, male parolees had higher return rates than females. Eighty-six percent of females survived the first year, compared to 77 percent for males released on parole. By the end of thirty-six months, nearly 50 percent of the males compared to 36 percent of females who received PMA time had returned to prison.

The distribution by age is also consistent with prior findings. The youngest age group (eighteen to twenty-two) has the lowest survival probabilities. Older parolees (thirty-three and older) have the highest survival rates, though the oldest category of parolees experienced a slight downturn.

The survival patterns by race/ethnicity are somewhat different from the results reported in chapter 4. As in other cohorts, African-American parolees have the lowest survival rates of all three race/ethnic groups. After the end of three years, 55 percent of these parolees were back in prison. By comparison, Anglo survival probabilities are substantially higher, especially after three years. By the end of thirty-six months, 45 percent of Anglo parolees were returned to TDC. The departure from findings reported for earlier cohorts is that Latinos in the PMA cohort had a slightly higher survival rate than their Anglo counterparts.

Finally, the distribution of parole success by assessed risk is very dramatic. Fully 37 percent of those assessed to be high-risk parolees were reincarcerated in the first twelve months. Sixty-one percent failed by the end of the second year. After three years, nearly 70 percent were back in

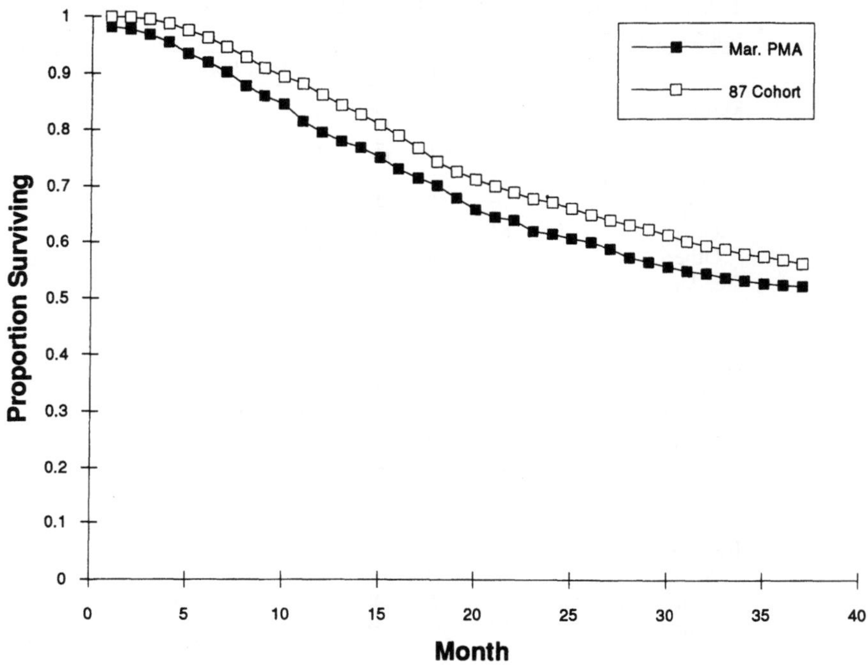

FIGURE 6.1. Survival curves for the march PMA and 1987 cohorts.

prison. High-risk parolees experienced the greatest increase in failure in the first year. While they continue to fail in the second and third years, the rate of increase in reincarceration slows somewhat. Medium- and low-risk releasees have survival rates that decline more slowly compared to their high-risk counterparts. By the end of the third year, 53 percent of medium-risk and 65 percent of low-risk parolees survived.

The decline in parole success for high-risk PMA releasees is the most pronounced of all of the cohorts we have studied. In this sense, there is some evidence that the PMA releases were more likely to be recidivists. It is, of course, important to make additional comparisons before reaching any final conclusions.

Figure 6.1 presents the thirty-six month trends in the cumulative proportion surviving for both cohorts. As is evident, the PMA cohort had consistently lower survival probabilities throughout the follow-up period. After twelve months, 78 percent of the PMA cohort had survived, compared to 84 percent of the baseline cohort. After twenty-four months, the comparable figures are 61 percent and 66 percent. Finally, after three years on parole, 52 percent of the PMA cohort survived compared to 56 percent of the non-PMA cohort.

TABLE 6.1. Survival rates for the PMA and Non-PMA release cohorts.

	PMA			Non-PM		
Months	12	24	36	12	24	36
Total	78	61	52	84	66	56
Release offense						
Property	76	57	49	83	63	53
Drug	83	70	61	88	71	63
Other	75	59	50	89	70	61
Gender						
Male	77	59	51	84	65	55
Female	86	73	64	91	77	65
Age						
18–22	71	53	42	74	54	44
23–27	78	62	53	82	64	52
28–32	75	56	49	85	63	54
33–37	81	66	58	88	71	62
38–42	88	71	63	94	77	72
43+	80	68	62	91	79	70
Race/ethnicity						
Anglo	79	63	55	86	69	62
African-American	73	55	45	81	61	48
Latino	82	65	58	85	69	59
Assessed risk						
High	63	39	31	78	53	42
Medium	78	61	53	83	63	53
Low	87	74	65	91	79	72

Thus, the greatest difference between the PMA and baseline cohorts occurs in the first twelve months following release. Thereafter, the rates of returning tend to converge. The plot of the respective hazard rates confirms this differential timing of parole failure. Figure 6.2 presents the six-month moving average of the hazard rates for the two cohorts. The rates for both cohorts tend to peak at approximately the same points—months fourteen and sixteen. The trend for the baseline 1987 cohort is one of monotonically increasing hazards from the first to the fourteenth month and then a fairly consistent decline from that point on. While the PMA cohort parallels part of this pattern, there are important differences. The hazards for the PMA cohort begin at a higher level throughout the first year. After the early part of the second year after release, the rates move in a reasonably parallel fashion.

Another way of comparing these two groups is through the use of survival prediction models. These models are the same type of lognormal parametric models explored in chapter 5. The dependent variable is the length of time from parole release to reincarceration and includes censored observations. The predictor variables are age, assessed risk, gender, prior incarceration offense, and race/ethnicity.

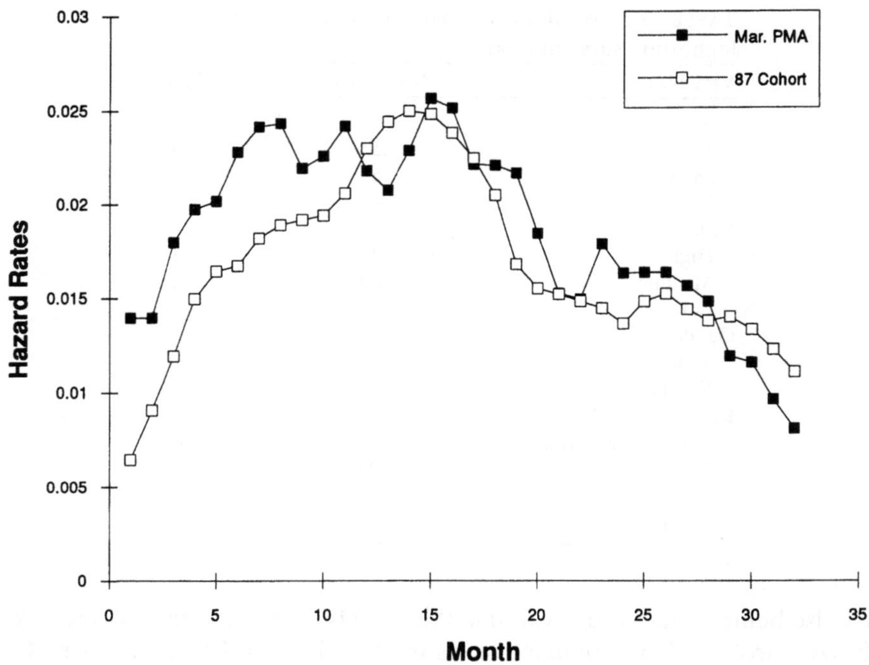

FIGURE 6.2. Hazard rates for the March PMA and 1987 cohorts.

Table 6.2 presents the antilogs of the parameter estimates for the two release cohorts for the variables that are significant. The results for the PMA cohort are identical to the results for the non-PMA cohort in terms of statistically significant variables—age, assessed risk, gender, and race/ethnicity. However, there are important differences in terms of the magnitude of the effects.

Recall that the interpretation of the exponentiated coefficients is in terms of the proportion of survival time for a particular group compared to the reference group. Thus, the coefficient of .55 for non-PMA parolees in the eighteen to twenty-seven age group means that net of the other variables included in the model, those who are eighteen to twenty-seven have a survival time that is on average only 55 percent of parolees thirty-eight and over (the reference group).

The PMA and non-PMA cohorts do not differ with regard to the effect of age. Both groups have nearly equal coefficients, with the youngest age group exhibiting the lowest survival time. The gender effect is somewhat stronger for PMA releasees as is the effect of race/ethnicity. Male and African-American PMA releasees have a lower expected survival time compared to their non-PMA counterparts. The most dramatic difference, however, is with regard to assessed risk. High-risk PMA releasees have,

TABLE 6.2. Antilogs of parameter estimates from lognormal survival models.

Variables	Non-PMA	PMA
Age		
18–27	.55	.54
28–32	.66	.58
32+	—	—
Risk		
High	.44	.31
Medium	.60	.72
Low	—	—
Gender		
Male	.69	.60
Female	—	—
Race/ethnicity		
African-American	.77	.62
Latino	1.04	1.14
Anglo	—	—
Intercept	175	135

all else being equal, a survival time that is only 31 percent that of low-risk PMA parolees. The comparable figure for the non-PMA group is 44 percent.

A useful way to summarize the differences between these two cohorts is to estimate the expected time from release to return for parolees with characteristics that are associated with a high likelihood of return, i.e., being eighteen to twenty-seven years of age, high-risk, male, and African-American. The predicted time from release to return is obtained by adjusting the intercept by multiplying it times the coefficient for each of these characteristics. Thus, for the non-PMA cohort, this involves multiplying 175 (the intercept) by .55 (the coefficient for 18 to 27), then multiplying that product by .44 (the high-risk coefficient), then multiplying that product by .69 (the coefficient for males), and finally multiplying by .76 (for African-Americans). The expected average time from release to return for non-PMA parolees with these characteristics is 22.6 months. A counterpart PMA parolee who is between eighteen and twenty-seven, male, high-risk, and African-American has an average time from release to reincarceration of only 8.8 months. The differential in the predicted return time reflects the substantial difference across these two cohorts in not only the level but also the timing of return.

The most obvious explanation for the differences between the PMA and non-PMA cohorts is compositional. Table 6.3 presents the percentage distributions of parolee characteristics for the two release cohorts. The PMA cohort is essentially identical to the general cohort with regard to gender and race/ethnicity. The PMA cohort is slightly younger (19 percent between the ages of 18 and 22 compared to 15 percent for the baseline

TABLE 6.3. Distribution of parolee characteristics for the PMA and Non-PMA release cohorts.

Variables	PMA	Non-PMA
Release offense		
Violent	0	17
Property	67	54
Drug	24	18
Other	8	11
Gender		
Male	91	91
Female	9	9
Age		
18–22	19	15
23–27	26	27
28–32	24	24
33–37	16	17
38–42	7	8
43+	8	10
Race/ethnicity		
Anglo	42	42
African-American	36	38
Latino	22	20
Assessed risk		
High	15	12
Medium	65	63
Low	20	25

cohort). The PMA cohort is also more high risk—15 percent compared to 12 percent. Predictably, the major compositional difference is with regard to prior incarceration offense. The PMA cohort has substantially more releasees with prior property offenses—67 percent compared to 54 percent. Another difference related to prior incarceration offense is the absence of violent offenders in the PMA cohort. Based on these compositional differences, we would predict higher return-to-prison rates for the PMA cohort.

Do these and perhaps other compositional differences between the two cohorts fully account for the differences in survival probabilities? Table 6.1 (presented above) addresses this question by presenting the proportion surviving for both cohorts at the three twelve-month intervals, broken down by parolee characteristics. If compositional differences fully account for the differences in survival rates, then the proportion surviving *within* categories of parolee characteristics should not differ much across cohorts. However, notable differences are evident. For example, the proportion surviving at twelve, twenty-four, and thirty-six months for parolees with property offenses is lower for the PMA cohort (76, 57, and 49 percent respectively, compared to 83, 63, and 53 percent for the baseline cohort).

Although there are no compositional differences by gender, the proportion surviving is different for males and females when comparing the PMA to the non-PMA cohort. Differences by age do not appear very dramatic at the younger ages but do increase as parolee age increases (those twenty-eight and older). There is a similar differential with regard to race/ethnicity. Anglo and African-American survival rates differ across cohorts with a greater differential for African-Americans. Latino survival rates do not differ much when comparing PMA with non-PMA releases.

The most dramatic differentials when comparing cohorts are evident across risk categories. Specifically, high-risk PMA releasees have substantially lower survival rates compared to their counterparts in the 1987 baseline cohort. At twelve months, high-risk PMAs have survival probabilities fifteen percentage points lower than non-PMA releasees. At twenty-four months, the differential is fourteen percentage points, and after three years, it is eleven percentage points. The differences are narrower for medium- and low-risk releasees. Thus, as noted earlier, the differences in return rates for high-risk parolees in the two cohorts occur almost entirely during the first year. Thereafter, the differential narrows.

It is clear that part of the overall differential in survival between the PMA and non-PMA cohorts is due to the composition of these two groups. This finding in and of itself is very important. However, that is not the end of the story. Why do differences in survival probabilities remain when we compare *within* categories? In particular, why are parolees assessed as high risk among the PMA releasees more likely to return to prison than their counterparts in the non-PMA cohort?

An obvious potential answer hinges on whether high-risk PMA parolees were, on average, higher risks than their non-PMA counterparts? We assessed this possibility by computing the average risk scores for the high-risk category. Remembering that a lower score means a higher risk, a comparison of the average risk scores for the PMA and non-PMA cohorts reveal statistically significant differences. The average risk score for parolees judged to be high risk in the 1987 baseline cohort is 2.94. The comparable mean risk score for the PMA cohort is 1.90, indicating that the high-risk PMA parolees were determined to be higher risk than their counterparts who left prison a month earlier. It is this heightened risk among the high-risk parolees that may account, at least in part, for the lower survival rates among the March PMA parolees. This finding is consistent with the argument that the Parole Board was forced to further scrape the bottom of the barrel in order to remain within the guidelines of the PMA legislation and thereby remain in compliance with *Ruiz*.

The PMA legislation was designed to release inmates perceived as posing less of a public safety *threat*. In general, this meant that offenders convicted of violent offenses and offenses against children were excluded from early release consideration. On the other hand this same legislation was designed to accecerate the release of property offenders. These offenders, while less *threatening*, were more *risky* when it came to the probability of recidivism and, thus, reincarceration. It appears that the pressure on the Parole Board to identify and release inmates under the provisions of the PMA resulted in the increased release of inmates who by definition had a higher likelihood of return to prison.

Although compositional differences between the PMA and non-PMA parolees go a long way toward accounting for the differentials in survival and hazard rates, there is reason to believe and some evidence to support the idea that factors other than compositional effects also played a significant role. For example, the early release process set in motion by the PMA may have sent a message to parolees that the prison crowding crisis was forcing the state to reduce punishments. We have seen some evidence (chapter 4) suggesting that this possibility may have been operating in the repetitious offending patterns among property offenders. While we were eventually able to explain much of this difference in terms of factors other than reduced deterrence, a differential remained. To further explore the possibility of a reduced deterrent effect, we return to comparisons of the PMA and non-PMA cohorts.

The trend in heightened repetitious property offending continued. Seventy percent of parolees in the general 1987 non-PMA cohort who

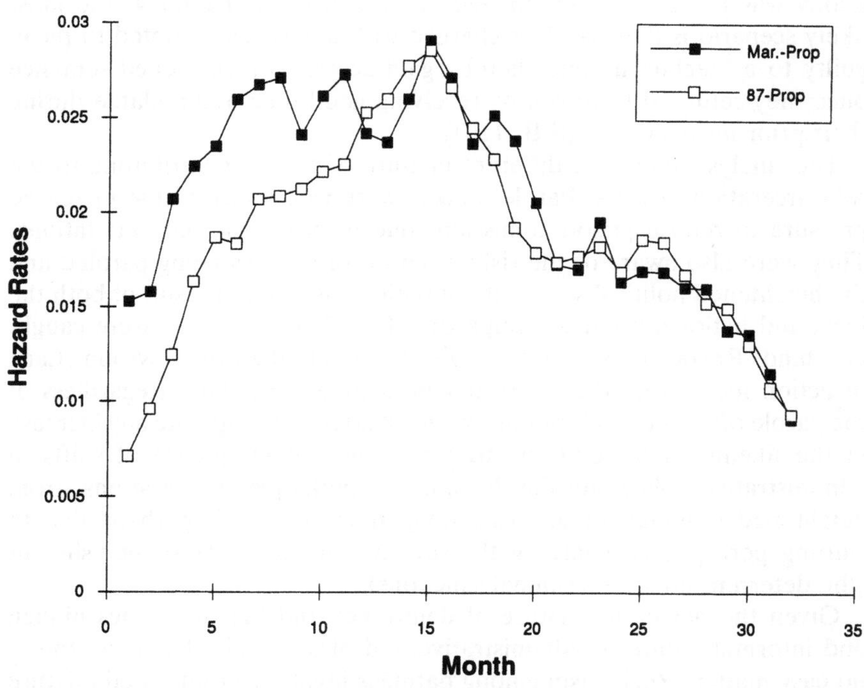

FIGURE 6.3. Hazard rates for the property offenders of March PMA and 87 cohorts.

had served sentences for property offenses returned to prison within three years for another property offense. The comparable figure for the March PMA cohort is 85 percent. Once again, while indirect, the evidence is consistent with a reduced deterrent effect. We will have occasion to return to this topic in the next two chapters. For now we focus on the what can be gained through further examination of survival and hazard rate curves.

Figure 6.3 focuses on hazard rates for property offenders. Since the majority of the releasees in the two cohorts are property offenders, the hazard rate curves resemble those for the cohorts as a whole. That is, the PMA property offenders, similar in ways to what we found among the 1986 cohort parolees in chapter 4, have a rapid, early rise in the hazard of returning to prison during the first year. After that point, the trends in the rates are quite similar.

Whatever differences there were in the two cohorts of property offenders—compositional, administrative, deterrence, or otherwise—resulted in higher return rates during approximately the first nine months. Thereafter, persons in both cohorts tended to return to prison at approximately the same rate. As discussed in previous chapters, persons returned to prison during the very early months of release were most likely to have been returned for technical violations. This does not mean that a new felony was not committed. Indeed, as discussed in chapter 4, the most likely scenario is that parolees charged with a new felony opted to plead guilty to a "technical" and thereby gain access to a shortened sentence once they returned to prison by receiving good time accumulated during their prior incarceration (S.B. 1167).

This analysis implies a different mixture of factors contributing to the reincarceration process. Parole officers were well aware of the increased pressure to reduce prison admissions due to prison capacity limitations. They were also aware of the riskier nature of persons being paroled and the heightened political sensitivity of their decisions as a result of both the local and national political campaigns of 1987. Hence, they were caught in a bind. Revocations meant charges of refilling the prison system. Lack of action meant that they were not protecting the public. Regardless of the parole officers considerations, we must attempt to separate any increase in the likelihood of returning to prison, as a consequence of shifts in administrative policy and the dynamics of guilty-plea negotiations, from heightened criminal tendencies among those released, perhaps due to shifting perceptions regarding the severity and certainty of punishment (the deterrent effect of criminal sanctions).

Given the perceptual nature of deterrence and the sometimes hidden and informal nature of administrative and plea-bargain decisions, this is no easy matter. Recidivism among parolees involves a rather odd mixture of what have been called general and specific deterrence factors. As far as general deterrence operates, parolees are susceptible to the same perceptions and evaluations of the sanctioning process as the general public. If punishment is heightened or the probability of imprisonment is reduced, they should be affected accordingly. The major difference between parolees and the general public is that parolees have more direct information on how sanctions have impinged on their own lives as well as on how the process is most likely to operate currently and in the near future. Thus, the salience of deterrence factors should be higher among parolees than among the general public.

The question that draws our attention in this chapter is whether, among persons who had received an unexpected reduction in their punishment due to early release, there was any noticeable increase in the chances of returning to prison and, if there was an increase, whether it can be attributed to a reduced deterrent effect as opposed to shifting administrative revocation policies or cohort composition effects.

Not having direct access to the mind-set of either the parole officers or offenders, we used the following substitute procedure. We first removed from consideration those who returned to prison during the first nine months (to level administrative revocation and guilty-plea differences) and then those assessed to be high risk (to level compositional differences).

Figure 6.4 reports the post-nine-month hazard rates among all releasees. With some slight variation early on, the two curves basically

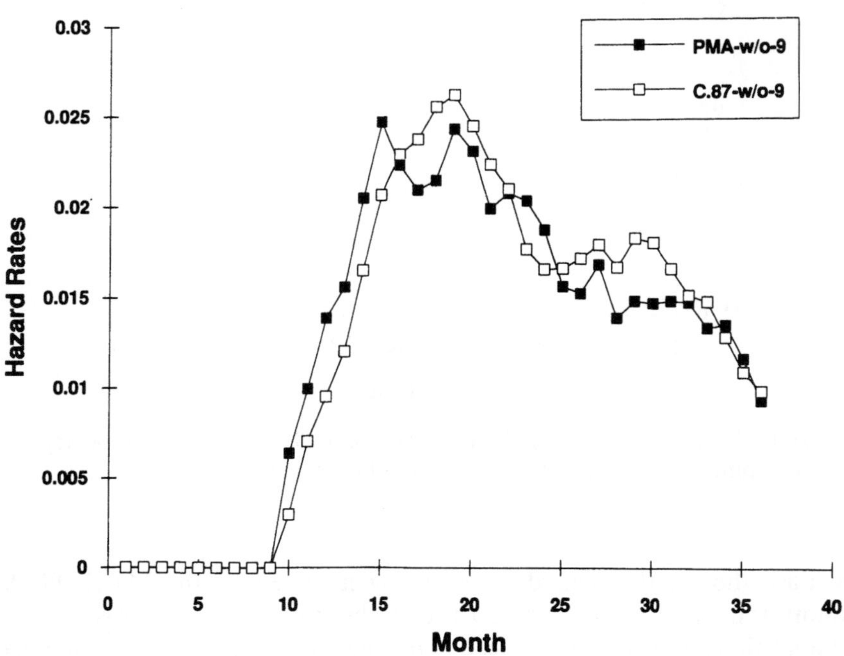

FIGURE 6.4. Hazard rates for March PMA and 1987 cohorts, omitting those returning in first 9 months.

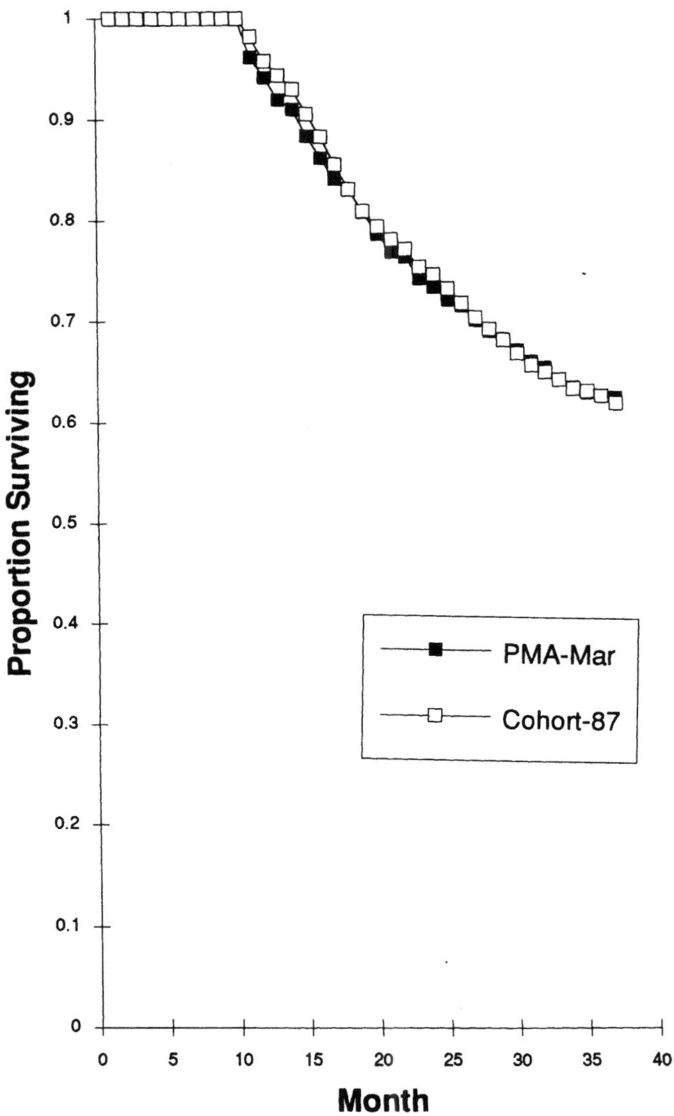

FIGURE 6.5. Survival curves for March PMA and 1987 cohorts for property offenders omitting high risk and failures within first 9 months.

overlap, though the hazard rates among members of the March PMA cohort remain a bit higher. To see if this remaining gap was due to compositional effects as evidenced in the higher average risk scores among high-risk parolees or to heightened criminal tendencies, especially among property offenders encouraged by reduced deterrence, we removed high-risk parolees from both cohorts and restricted comparisons to parolees who had been released after serving sentences for property offenses. These survival rate results are reported in figure 6.5. As is evident, this method of leveling the cohorts removed all remaining differences. This result indicates the importance of compositional differences as an explanation of the variation across these cohorts released one month apart in 1987.

At the same time, it is important to remember the heightened probability of return to prison in the early months of release in the PMA cohort. This finding underscores the idea that parole officers and offenders alike were responding to changes taking place in the administration of justice in Texas during these years. Whether this reflects a reduced deterrent effect, some administrative policy shift, or perhaps other forces in the broader social and economic climate of the time is a topic to be taken up in the next chapter.

Conclusion

We have provided evidence supporting all three of the explanations we developed for the observed differences in the PMA and non-PMA survival and hazard-rate trends. Compositional differences between the PMA and non-PMA cohorts account in part for the differential patterns. It is also possible that the PMA had some impact on the deterrent effect of incarceration. Evaluation of the hazard rate trends for the two cohorts (figure 6.2) also suggests that PMA parolees had a higher likelihood of being returned to prison on a technical violation in the early months following release. The heightened hazard rates in the first year, especially during the first several months of the first year, indicate that those returned were probably not being processed through the courts with a new trial for a new offense but were being revoked for violating conditions of parole. It may have been that parole officers were more vigilant in supervising PMA releasees, perhaps because they were aware of the increased likelihood of recidivism associated with those eligible for PMA release. It may have been that the early processing more directly reflected the offenders' attempts to secure the sentencing advantages associated with S.B. 1167.

While the intent of the PMA was to release selected inmates to comply with *Ruiz*, our research indicates that there were serious unintended consequences. In the attempt to balance political considerations (not releasing inmates perceived to be threats to public safety) with the practical need to free up prison space, the legislature created a statute that contributed to the prison crowding crisis by speeding up the cycle time of release and return. To our knowledge, this analysis of the Texas case provides the first evidence that early release programs designed like the

PMA may in fact aggravate the problem they are designed to alleviate. At the same time, it is important to note that, given the crowding crisis and the threat of astronomical fines in the context of a severely strained state economy, the PMA did give state leaders and prison officials a bit of breathing space.

Continued use of the Texas PMA must be evaluated with caution, according to our findings. Parole officials must recognize that the "PMA pool" of inmates poses the hightened risk of recidivism that we have indicated. There is some evidence that current practices "flush" the PMA pool of inmates during crisis periods, without using the special review procedures associated with the PMA trigger clause. Parole officials have treated the PMA as a general signal by the legislature to target the PMA pool in their daily work of making release decisions.[6] Early release programs like that implemented in Texas need to be carefully evaluated in terms of the *longer term* consequences for prison crowding (e.g. Austin 1986). This recommendation is especially salient in light of the increasing popularity of these programs throughout the nation.

---

[6] Interview with Dr. Pablo Martinez, of the Texas Board of Pardons and Paroles, September 1, 1991.

7
Incarceration and Crime: Is There a Link?

Incarceration and Crime

Systematic research on the link between incarceration and crime rates began in the late 1960s and continued with increased momentum throughout the 1970s and 1980s. In response to a vigorous national debate over this research and over the appropriate role of criminal sanctions in reducing high-crime rates, a panel was convened in the late 1970s by the National Academy of Sciences (Blumstein, Cohen, and Nagin 1978) to systematically evaluate data then available.

The resulting report, *Deterrence and Incapacitation: Estimating the Effects of Criminal Sanctions on Crime Rates*, concluded, "We cannot yet assert that the evidence warrants an affirmative conclusion regarding deterrence." Nevertheless, the panel noted in cautious language that the preponderance of evidence favored a tentative proposition asserting a deterrent effect. Daniel Nagin, in one of the panel's commissioned papers, wrote:

> In this critique over 20 published analyses are cited, and even this list is less than exhaustive. Yet, despite the intensity of the research effort, the empirical evidence is still not sufficient for providing a rigorous confirmation of the existence of a deterrent effect. Perhaps more important, the evidence is woefully inadequate for providing a good estimate of the magnitude of whatever effect may exist. . . . Thus, policy suggestions, based upon the existing evidence, can only be made with a clear recognition of the inadequacy of the evidence. Accordingly, such suggestions must be very limited and posed with great caution.

Shortly after this report was issued, California launched what would become a colossally expensive quadrupling of its prison capacity during the 1980s. This building program was coupled with other significant changes as well (Austin 1989). The California legislature passed legislation in 1977 eliminating indeterminate sentencing by formally stating that the purpose of a prison sentence was punishment and not rehabilitation. Under the new sentencing scheme, convicted felons were to receive fixed sentences that could only be reduced by earning various forms of good-time credits while in prison.

Laws were also enacted that increased penalties for offenders and at the same time reduced options available to the judicial system. For example, between 1980 and 1982, sentences for felony residential burglary became mandatory as well as more severe. This legislation along with Proposition 8, which became known as the Victims' Bill of Rights, exemplified changes in the administration of criminal justice that had an impact on the California Department of Corrections in terms of increased admissions as well as longer sentences (California Department of Corrections 1984).

These historic legislative changes were likely motivated by two factors. One is the idea that prison has a direct effect on the ability of offenders to commit additional crimes, i.e., the function of incapacitation. The second factor is deterrence. One of the central elements of deterrence theory is the certainty and severity of punishment. Determinate sentencing, coupled with the increased capacity to incarcerate, may have increased both the certainty and severity of punishment in California in comparison to other states such as Texas that relied primarily on indeterminate sentencing and parole.

With incapacitation and increased prison capacity, the impact of incarceration on the crime rate is seemingly more obvious. If offenders are put in prison, they are prevented, for that time, from committing further crimes in the community. Such an obviously direct connection led James Q. Wilson, to write *Thinking About Crime* (1975)—a widely read book—which advocates determinate sentencing policies, claiming "the gains from merely incapacitating convicted criminals may be very large . . . and if the policy of prison sentences were consistently followed, even with relatively short (one or two years) sentences, the gains would be enduring." (1975, 193–94). While this conclusion is appealingly straightforward, further reflection yields a more complicated picture. It is one thing to say that a particular person will not commit a crime against the community while incarcerated and quite another to say that community crime rates will be affected.

One important complicating factor that arises when assessing the link between incapacitation and the community crime rate is that criminals can be replaced. As Gottfredson and Hirschi (1990) have convincingly argued, although most criminal behavior is not organized in any usual sense of that term, there is some crime (for example, car-theft rings and fencing stolen property [Klockars 1974] or distributing illegal drugs [Ekland-Olson et al. 1984]), that is organized much like a labor market. In these instances, when an arrest is made, a conviction secured, and a prison sentence imposed, a vacancy comes open. This vacancy may be filled with little delay, and thus the rate of crime can continue without interruption. To date, there has been no systematic estimation of this labor market/job replacement model when it comes to the impact of incapacitation. It may be that all incapacitation does in the long term is expand the pool of experienced labor.

Setting aside this unanswered research question, there are other assumptions built into the idea that incapacitation will reduce the general crime rate, all of which demand empirical confirmation of a seemingly simple idea. Fortunately, there is available research to draw upon (e.g., Greenberg 1975; Clarke 1974; Cohen 1978; Greenwood 1983; Conrad 1985).

Employing a number of simplifying assumptions and statistical estimation procedures, Clarke concluded that even if we doubled the number of juvenile offenders incarcerated, we would realize a reduction in the index crime rate of only approximately 1 to 4 percent. Interestingly, Greenberg (1975), using a different methodology in a study of adult felons in California, reached a similar reduction-in-crime estimate of just under 5 percent, assuming a 50 percent increase (from two to three years on average) in sentence lengths. In her review of these studies, Jacqueline Cohen (1978) conjectured that both Greenberg and Clarke had underestimated the incapacitation effect of incarceration, but that the mistake was not very large. In any case, none of the early studies confirmed a reduction in the crime rate close to the reduction posited by Wilson in the original edition of *Thinking About Crime*.

In an attempt to focus the issue more precisely, a group of researchers at Ohio State University led by John Conrad and Simon Dinitz, carried out what came to be known as the Dangerous Offenders Project. Numerous monographs were eventually written, reporting a series of studies designed to assess the effect of incapacitation on offenders convicted of murder, rape, robbery, and aggravated assault. Overall, these researchers were rather pessimistic about the potential of incapacitation as a means to reduce the rate of violent crime.

For example Van Dine, Conrad, and Dinitz (1979, 43) concluded the following:

> Many of these individuals must have committed their offenses as impulsive responses to the situation confronting them, sometimes under the distortions of alcohol or drugs, sometimes by a transitory loss of control in a condition of fear or anger. No incapacitation policy is going to prevent many crimes committed under these circumstances. It is likely that our cohort is fairly representative of experience elsewhere, and that a large number of the violent crimes cleared by the police are of this character—first offenses committed under stresses and influences inaccessible to the preventive processes of the law.

Still, the crime-reducing appeal of incapacitation remains (Zedlewski 1987; Langan 1991). The conclusions of Van Dine, Conrad, and Dinitz stand up if we assume that violent crimes come from nonchronic offenders and are situationally encouraged with the help of alcohol and drugs. But, might there be some offenders with more stable patterns of violence who could be selectively incapacitated?

The best early evidence that much of the crime rate came from a relatively small group of chronic offenders is available from a study of the records of 10,000 boys in Philadelphia (Wolfgang, Figlio, and Sellin 1972). In this study of a birth cohort, it was found that one-sixth of the delinquents were responsible for more than half of the offenses committed by all delinquents.

While the idea that most of the trouble comes from a relatively small segment of the population was certainly not new, the policy implications of this Philadelphia birth cohort study were recognized almost immediately. In particular, the study stimulated the pursuit of a policy wherein we turn from preventive efforts aimed at the population as a whole toward those aimed at a much smaller proportion of the population thought to be responsible for a disproportionate share of crime—in short, toward selective incapacitation.

The proposed advantages of such a policy were many. Gottfredson and Hirschi (1990, 259), in an otherwise critical review, examined some of the implications:

> . . . with minimal money and effort, sizable reductions in the crime rate can be achieved. Since the focus is on chronic, habitual, or career criminals, there would be few legal or ethical problems with a policy that isolates them from society. Since the number of career criminals is small, it may be possible to reduce the scope of the criminal justice system at all levels, from police to prisons. Instead of a large and unwieldy system passively accepting a mixture of occasional, petty, and serious offenders, this new policy would create an efficient system where resources could be focused on the dangerous few. Finally, this new system would take the criminal justice system out of the business of dealing with social problems and put it to work doing what it alone can do: identifying and removing from circulation people whose continued freedom would jeopardize the safety of the community.

Success in realizing these proposed advantages depends on identifying who should be selectively incapacitated. Two approaches were eventually pursued. The first depended on statistical prediction, the second on community tolerance. Accuracy, along with ethical and legal problems, would stymie the first. Escalating prison construction costs would plague the second.

Attempts to statistically predict criminal behavior predate the current interest in selective incapacitation by more than two decades (e.g., McCord and McCord 1959). The record of success is not impressive (Thornberry and Jacoby 1979; Monahan 1981; Morris and Miller 1985; Tonry 1987). The most important problem is the presence of "false positive" predictions—predictions that persons will engage in criminal behavior when in fact they do not.

Difficulties not withstanding, Peter Greenwood (1983) launched an ambitious effort to identify high-rate offenders. In interviews with inmates housed in prisons and jails in California, Texas, and Michigan, Greenwood asked persons to report crimes they had committed during the two years immediately preceding their current incarceration. From these interviews he developed a seven-item scale for predicting high-rate offenders.

Criticism, including self-criticism by Greenwood and Turner (1987), of this prediction scale and philosophy of punishment was immediate and enduring, (e.g., Cohen 1983; Blackmore and Welsh 1983; Chaiken and Chaiken 1984; von Hirsch 1985; and Gottfredson and Hirschi 1990). False positives were noted to be as high as 50 percent, hardly a level acceptable to deny liberty in any program of selective incapacitation. The scale depended on self-reports, which are not a means to inspire confidence when the person reporting knows his or her sentence depends on the answers given. The scale was too little and too late. By the time persons were tagged by the scale, they would be well into their criminal careers and perhaps even "aging out." Therefore, the scale would be effective too late for any real reduction in the crime rate.

While the problems stemming from inaccurate, dilatory predictions are important, they are not the end of the story. Selective incapacitation, based as it is on predictions about future behavior, runs into substantial ethical and legal difficulties as well (Tonry 1987). Most obviously, scales designed to guide selective incapacitation decisions allow sentencing on the basis of what we think persons will do in the future rather than on the conviction offense. Proponents of the practice are quick to respond that there is ample legal precedent. For example, the Supreme Court has held that the Texas Capital Punishment statute is constitutional even though it hinges on predictions made by the jury that the defendant constitutes a continuing violent threat to society (Marquart, Ekland-Olson, and Sorenson 1989).

Clearly, whatever the philosophy of punishment, all persons are interested in accurate predictions. What if we add variables to improve our predictions? Males are more likely to be violent, as are younger persons and persons from some ethnic and racial groups tend to be more violent than others. Does this mean that benefits of selective incapacitation can legitimize practices that in other circumstances would be called racist, sexist, or age-biased? Most would answer this inquiry with a resounding no. Hence, the dilemma. We want to limit crime, especially violent crime, but our predictions are inaccurate. In our quest to improve accuracy, we raise troublesome ethical and legal problems.

Confronted with this dilemma, states have turned from the empirical, legal, and ethical constraints of prediction models as a means to achieve selective incapacitation to broad-based, nonselective incapacitation based on crimes (not criminals) and community tolerance. Mandatory determinate sentences for criminal acts thought to be particularly threatening—for example, offenses involving violence or drug trafficking—have come increasingly into vogue. While evident in many states, this tendency is nowhere more apparent than in California, where the trend began in the late 1970s and early 1980s (Austin 1989; Zimring 1990).

The question becomes whether the tendency toward incarceration and deterrence is linked to any systematic changes in the crime rate. It is said that no one engages in social research free from personal bias. We are no exception. We began this project to assess dramatic changes in the administration of justice with some skepticism regarding the influence that incarceration and prison capacity have on the crime rate. As the above suggests, we were not alone in this skepticism. We now turn to some comparative analyses that help shed further light on the subject.

National and Two-State Comparisons

There is no doubt that since the mid-1970s we have seen what is universally described as explosive growth in the nation's prison population. On New Year's Eve 1989, according to Bureau of Justice Statistics, the nation's prison systems, both state and federal, housed just under 680,000 inmates (Bureau of Justice Statistics 1990). This was approximately three times the number incarcerated when the explosive growth in the prison population began in the 1970s and twice the number at the beginning of the 1980s. Counting only state prison systems, there were some 63,000 more inmates at the end of 1989 than at the same time the previous year. By the end of the 1980s, we were adding the equivalent of two five hundred-bed state facilities every six days nation wide.

Depending on whether these facilities were constructed of prefabricated concrete components as in Florida, or with more traditional methods, the estimated per-cell cost ranged from $16,000 to $50,000 (Petersilia and Turner 1986). In addition, the cost of day-to-day operations is estimated at something approaching $13,000 to $20,000 per inmate, per year, depending on what costs are included. Keeping in mind that much of the growth in the nation's incarcerated population came at the expense of increased crowding rather than new cells and that there is wide variation across states in per-inmate costs, the question remains, What have we purchased in terms of the crime rate?

There is considerable debate on the issue of the relationship between incarceration and the crime rate. As recently as November 1991, the *Houston Chronicle* ran an article entitled "Let's Lock Up More Criminals—It Works." The author states:

> One of America's best kept secrets is that our huge investment in building prisons—an estimated $30 billion in the last decade to double capacity—has

> produced a tremendous payoff: Americans are safer and, as the Justice Department reported a few days ago, crime has fallen steadily.
>
> Moreover, some pioneering research and police field testing suggest that if we again double the present federal and state prison population—to somewhere between 1 million and 1.5 million—and leave our city and county jail populations at the present 400,000, we will break the back of America's crime wave (Methuin 1991).

Using data from the National Crime Surveys, Langan (1991) provides a recent attempt to address this issue. While cautious, he finds some evidence for the beneficial return on the investment in prison capacity and incarceration. During the decade and a half between 1973 and 1989, Langan notes that the increase in the probability of incarceration ran parallel to a decrease in the national crime rate as measured by the National Crime Surveys. Recognizing that these parallel trends might be accounted for by a wide range of additional common determinants, he cautiously concludes, "If only one-half or even one-fourth of the reductions were the result of rising incarceration rates, that would still leave prisons responsible for sizable reductions in crime. That possibility must be seriously weighed in debates about America's prisons" (1573).

The national trend was partially driven by and certainly reflected in Texas and California. Both states experienced dramatic increases in their prison populations and incarceration rates between the mid-1970s and the late 1980s. However, California's prison population growth was, by far, more substantial. In large measure this was due to the adoption in California of a massive prison construction policy (Zimring 1990). Again, this construction effort was driven to a large extent by legislative changes in sentencing structure (the implementation of determinate, mandatory sentencing) and, as Austin (1989) has noted, an increase in parole revocations. In 1987, slightly over 50 percent of prison admissions in California were parole revocations.

By contrast, as we have seen in chapter 2, the Texas prison system began leveling off sometime in late 1986. This difference comparing these two states presents us with a natural experiment of sorts, with incarceration being the independent variable and crime rates the outcome.

Plotted in figure 7.1 are the total index crime rates, per 100,000 population, for Texas, California, and the U. S. as a whole from 1970 to 1989.[1] In the early part of the series (1970 to approximately 1979–80), the *trends* in the total index crime rates for Texas, California, and the U. S. were essentially the same—rising throughout most of the 1970s—

---

[1] It is important to note that the crime rate data reported here are based on the Uniform Crime Reports. For this reason, the trends reported here are not directly comparable with those reported by Langan (1991), whose analysis is based on the National Crime Surveys.

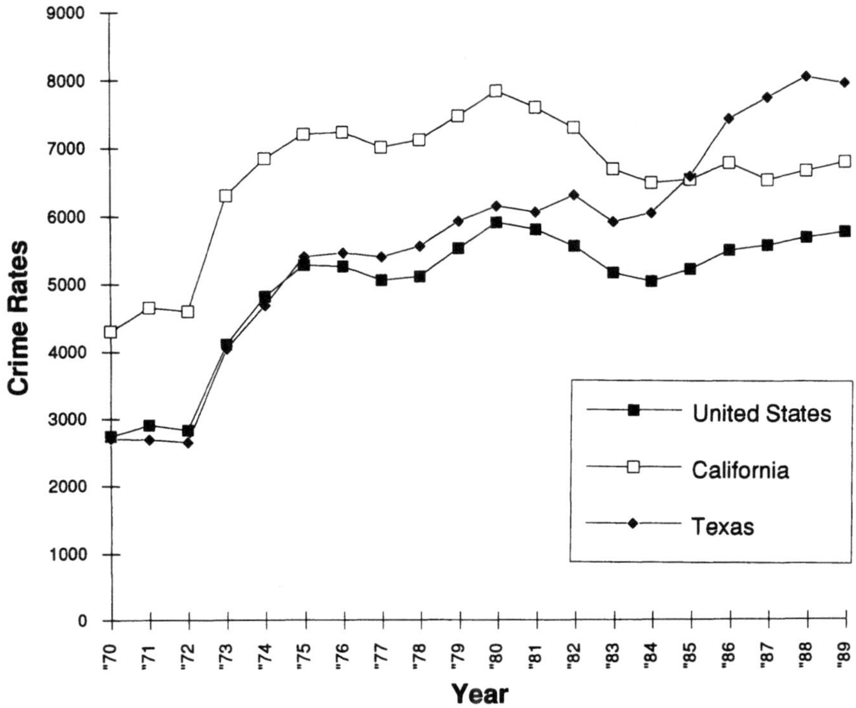

FIGURE 7.1. Total index crime rates for the U.S., California and Texas, 1970–1989.

although the California rates were considerably higher than those for the U. S. as a whole as well as Texas.

Beginning in 1980, the California crime rate began to decline. As a rough approximation, the crime rate in California, as reflected in the Uniform Crime Reports, was moving with the national rate, declining from 1980 to 1984–85 and then stabilizing or slightly increasing from 1985 to 1989. However, it is important to note that between 1980 and 1989, the national rate declined by 2.7 percent, whereas the California rates declined by 14 percent.

The trend in the Texas crime rate is almost a mirror image of the California trend. While the national and California rates began to decline in 1980, the Texas rates initially stabilized for a period of approximately three years. By 1984, the rate began to increase, and increase dramatically, surpassing California by 1986. The total index crime rates in Texas increased by nearly 30 percent between 1980 and 1989. Without further analysis, this comparison would indicate that the more ambitious prison construction policies in California may have been paying off.

While it is instructive to present trends in total index crimes, it is also important to disaggregate the total rates into violent and property offenses. Figure 7.2 presents the trends over the same period for violent index crimes. While the California violent crime rates are consistently higher than the national and Texas rates, the trends are, with minor exceptions, quite comparable. For the most part, the violent crime rates, as reflected in the Uniform Crime Reports, increase throughout the 1970s, decline from about 1980 to 1985, and then turn upward for the remainder of the 1980s. Taken by themselves, these data indicate that the money spent in California on prison construction was money wasted. The near-quadrupling of prison capacity seemed to make little difference when it came to curbing the rate of violent crime.

Figure 7.3 presents the 1970 to 1989 trend in property crimes for the United States, California, and Texas. The trend in property crimes was essentially the same for the nation, California, and Texas throughout the decade of the 1970s. However, by 1980, things began to change. California property crime rates *declined* 17 percent between 1980 and 1989. The Texas property crime rates *increased* by 30 percent. By the end of the 1980s, the Texas property crime rate was approximately 25 percent higher

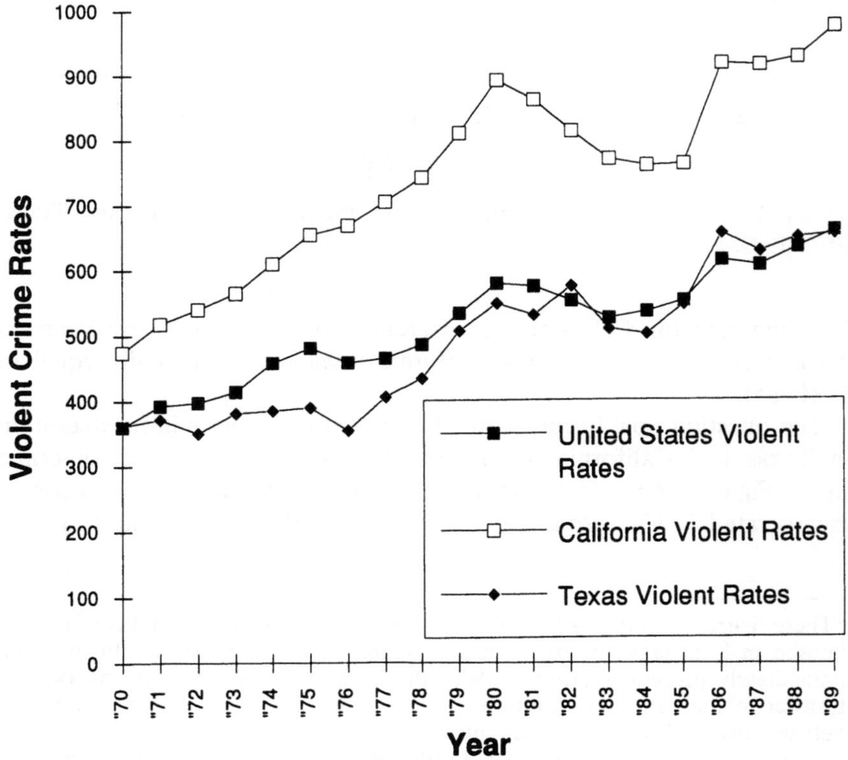

FIGURE 7.2. Violent index crime rates for the U.S., California and Texas, 1970 to 1989.

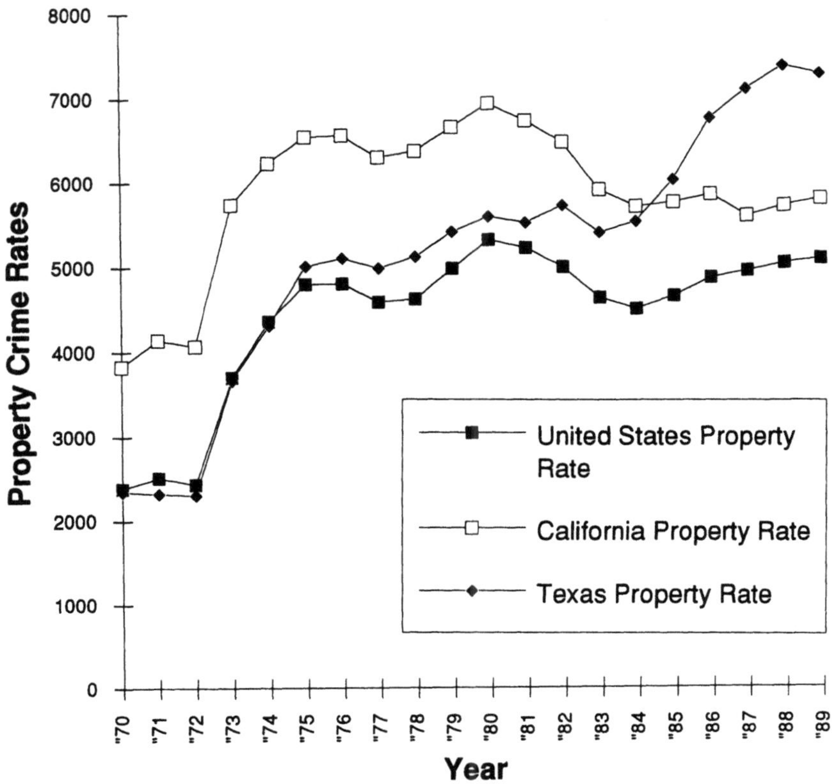

FIGURE 7.3. Property index crime rates for the U.S., California and Texas, 1970–1989.

than the rate for California, a differential that took only five years to achieve (i.e., the Texas and California rates were essentially equal in 1984–85).

The question now becomes to what extent differences in incarceration in Texas and California are related to the observed trends in crime rates. Figure 7.4 presents the annual trends in the number of prisoners incarcerated in California and Texas from 1970 to 1989.[2] The trends in

---

[2] These figures should be adjusted in the case of Texas with the number of persons housed in local jails, awaiting transfer to the state prison system. In the years immediately preceding October 1987, the backlog of convicted felons awaiting transfer to the various institutions in the Texas Department of Corrections was between two and three thousand inmates.

Beginning in October 1987 TDC instituted a controlled admission policy which resulted in an increase in this backlog. Between November 1987 and November 1990 quarterly readings were taken on this backlog, which reached a peak of

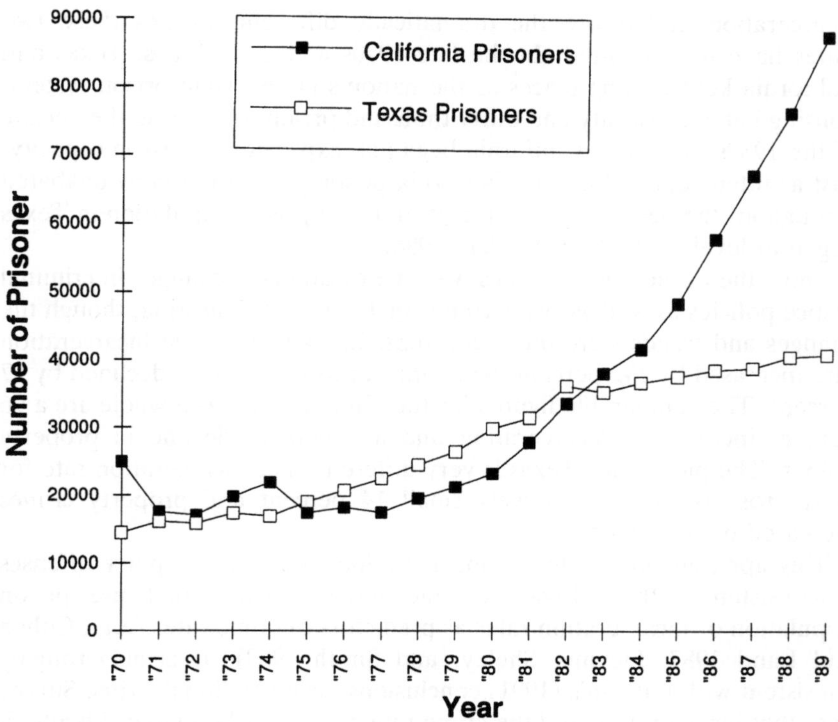

FIGURE 7.4. Total number of inmates incarcerated in state prisons in California and Texas, 1970–1989.

11,255 inmates in August of 1989. While this number is significant, it does not alter the basic point that growth in the California prison population (where there were also inmates awaiting transfer to state institutions) was dramatically greater than that experienced in Texas.

According to figures from the Board of Pardons and Paroles, the backlog figures for each reporting period were as follows:

November 87	3474
February 88	4227
May 88	4949
August 88	5649
November 88	7081
February 89	8103
May 89	10178
August 89	11255
November 89	10377
February 90	9946
May 90	7359
August 90	6183
November 90	6787

incarceration underscore the dramatically different policies these two states have implemented. In the late 1970s and early 1980s, Texas and California kept trading places as the nation's largest state prison system, housing between twenty and thirty thousand prisoners. During the decade of the 1980s, however, California began an expansion of prison capacity. Just as interesting, while the California prison population grew unabated throughout the decade by a factor of four, the prison population in Texas began to level off at 40,000 in late 1986.[3]

Thus, the decade of the 1980s was one of dramatic changes in criminal justice policies as well as crime trends in Texas and California, though the changes and trends were quite different. In California, the incarceration rate increased by 192 percent, while index property crimes declined by 17 percent. The comparable figures for the United States as a whole are a 96 percent increase in incarceration and a 4 percent decline in property crimes. The picture for Texas is very different. The incarceration rate for Texas rose by a comparatively small 14 percent and property crimes increased by 30 percent.

This apparent link between incarceration rates and property offenses is consistent with multivariate time series analyses that use prison population or incarceration rates as predictors of crime rates (e.g., Cohen and Land 1987; Devine, Sheley, and Smith 1988). It is also roughly consistent with Langan's (1991) conclusions, using National Crime Survey data that incarceration and the crime rate are inversely related. Finally, it is in line with expectations based on the increased rate of repetitious property offenses among the four cohorts we followed in our analyses, reported in chapter 4, and the PMA and non-PMA cohorts we analyzed in chapter 6.

In sharp contrast, violent offense trends reflect a different pattern. A comparison of incarceration and violent crime rates in Texas and California indicates no relationship. This apparent differential link between incarceration and crime rates is consistent with a good deal of prior research suggesting that whatever link there is between crime and incarceration, it is accentuated in the case of property offenses (e.g., Chiricos 1987).

Alternative Explanations for Varying Trends in California and Texas

When examining the link between incarceration and crime, there clearly are other factors that need to be considered. Demographic variables such as age, race/ethnicity, and migration may have come into play. While

[3] Ibid.

shifts in state and national demographics need to be carefully considered, there is little evidence that these factors changed dramatically enough to produce the 17 percent decline in property crimes in California and 30 percent increase in Texas (see Langan 1991). A parallel examination of individual characteristics in the previous chapters certainly suggests that attributes such as age or ethnicity did not account for the noted shifts across cohorts of parolees. Similarly, shifting demographics fail to account for the noted differences in the trends, when comparing property and violent offenses.

Another factor to consider is the economy. California experienced relative economic prosperity in the latter half of the decade of the 1980s while Texas was experiencing a sharp recession. The question is whether this difference in economic conditions provides an alternative explanation to incarceration rates for the trends in both property and violent offenses.

In an analysis of some sixty-three studies, Chiricos (1987) found that the link between unemployment and crime was conditioned by the type of crime involved. The studies reviewed reveal little if any consistent link between unemployment and violent crime rates. By contrast, property crime rates were more susceptible to unemployment patterns, even allowing for the contrasting theses in the literature regarding the effects of opportunity and motivation (Cantor and Land 1985; Cook and Zarkin 1985; Wilson and Cook 1985). There was evidence to suggest that it is the *change in the* level of unemployment, rather than the *absolute* level, which is most closely related to shifts in property offenses. In this latter instance, however, the body of research reviewed was only suggestive, posing a question left unresolved by available evidence.

In a tentative way, the comparison between incarceration, crime rates, and unemployment patterns in California and Texas during the 1980s allows us to pursue this issue at least one small step, and toward the conclusion that the economy-crime relation is a complex one. Figure 7.5 plots the trends in unemployment for Texas, California, and the United States.

These trends track each other fairly closely, although at different levels, until 1984, when the unemployment rate in Texas increases by nearly 50 percent in a period of just two years, and the national and California rates continue to decline throughout the remainder of the decade.

The sudden and sizable increase in unemployment in Texas is consistent with the rise in property crime rates in the mid-1980s. Moreover, the decline in unemployment at the national level and in California is reasonably consistent with the trend in property crime rates nationwide and in California. Thus, to some extent it appears that these descriptive data suggest a link between economic conditions and property crime. However, it is not at all clear how strong that link is. For example, while the sharp rise in unemployment in Texas between 1984 and 1986 is, once

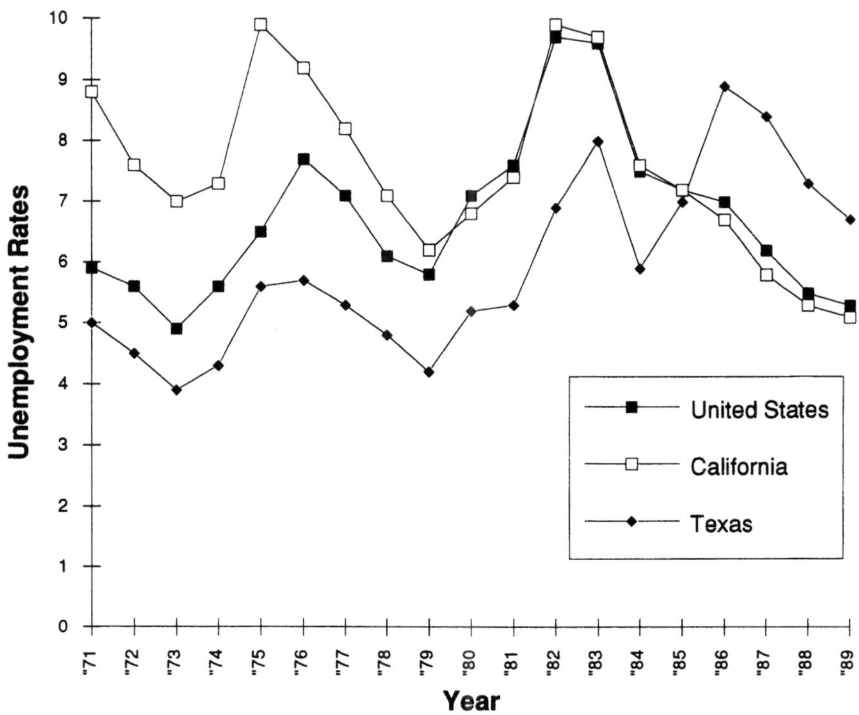

FIGURE 7.5. Unemployment rates for the U.S., California and Texas, 1971–1989.

again, consistent with the rise in property crime, we also note that the unemployment rate then declined by approximately 25 percent between 1986 and 1989, a period when property crimes continued to rise.

Conclusion

What can we say about the link between incarceration practices and crime rates, based on our findings as reported in earlier chapters and on this comparison of Texas and California? First, there were important differences in how California and Texas responded to pressure on the prison system during the 1980s. California embarked on a massive prison construction program and implemented significant changes in sentencing patterns. Texas opted for less construction and heavier reliance on parole release to manage the pressure on prison capacity.

Second, there were differences as well as similarities in crime rate trends in Texas and California. Violent crime rate *trends* were basically parallel throughout the years examined, although the California rates were considerably above those for Texas. Property crime rates exhibited quite different trends beginning in the mid-1980s, with the rates for Texas increasing significantly and the California rates declining and stabilizing. It is also important to note that the increase in property crimes in Texas is consistent with the increase in repetitious property offending across cohorts of parolees noted in chapter 4.

Finally, it is clear that there are contending explanations for the trends in crime rates. There appears to be some relationship between property crime and incarceration. There also appears to be a link between economic conditions and property crime rates. The most likely scenario is that it is the combination of factors that produced the very different property crime rate outcomes in Texas and California. In California, it was likely the combination of a healthy economy, increased prison capacity, and mandatory and determinate sentencing. In Texas, it was likely the combination of an economic recession, limited prison capacity, indeterminate sentencing, liberal allocation of good time, and legislation (S.B. 215 and H.B. 1167) that may have eroded any deterrent effect of incarceration.

8
Conclusions and Policy Implications

The decade of the 1980s was one of tremendous pressure on the criminal justice system. Criminologists, judges, prosecutors, and corrections officials alike concurred that prison crowding was the primary source of that pressure and thus the most critical problem facing the administration of criminal justice. By mid-decade, all but a handful of the states had directly experienced crowding in their prison facilities. Moreover, there was a virtual tidal wave of prisoner rights litigation in the federal courts, linked largely to crowded prison conditions. By 1986, over two-thirds of the states had become involved in lawsuits over the constitutionality of their prison systems. By the end of the decade forty-one states were under some form of court order regarding prison crowding.

Faced with a prison growth rate of nearly 185 percent between 1975 and 1989, as well as the intervention of the federal courts, states developed a variety of strategies for managing the prison crowding crisis. These strategies fall into one of three broad categories: remedies in the form of various diversion programs to reduce prison admissions; back-door solutions such as parole release; and capacity measures such as building programs and service expansion to enhance medical care, the staff-to-inmate ratio, as well as other resources that allowed administrators to handle an expanded number of inmates.

The Back-Door Solution: Parole Release

The previous chapters have explored in detail the back-door solution of the expanded use of parole. The criminal justice system in Texas went through tremendous changes during the decade of the 1980s. The prison population increased three-fold between the early 1970s and 1990, in part a result of increased crime, arrests, and convictions, but also as a consequence of an increased likelihood of prison sentences for convicted offenders. Federal court orders (*Ruiz v. Estelle*) resulted in caps being placed on the Texas prison population. Pressure was subsequently felt in criminal justice agencies throughout the state. The Texas legislature responded by placing much of the responsibility for managing the prison population crisis on the Board of Pardons and Paroles. The result was a massive increase in parole releases—345 percent growth between 1981 and 1990—that was facilitated by liberalized administrative good-time allocations and legislation that provided for accelerated early release. Moreover, the fact that 75 percent of the total prison population was paroled in one year (1991) provides further evidence of the scale of parole release in the state.

The primary question that motivated this research was the extent to which crime and, more specifically, the pattern and probability of reincarceration, was affected by these changes in the administration of criminal justice in Texas. In order to assess the impact of these changes, it was necessary to compile comparative, longitudinal data on four successive cohorts. Parolees in these cohorts were followed for a period of thirty-six months after release. These cohorts were selected to provide baseline data with which to compare parole outcomes as the prison crowding crisis intensified.

The results of our descriptive analyses in chapter 4 indicate that the two early cohorts (1984 and 1985) had essentially identical survival and hazard curves, comparable to national level trends. The later two cohorts (1986 and 1987) both had lower survival rates and distinctly different hazard rate curves. These results indicate that as the prison crisis intensified, changes took place in the patterns and probabilities of return to prison. The cohorts released during the peak of the crisis returned to prison not only at higher three-year probabilities but also more quickly.

In designing this study, we were not naive enough to believe that these data would shed much light on the question of deterrence, strictly defined. However, we were convinced that any observed patterns of parallel changes in the administration of criminal justice and reincarceration probabilities and patterns would be instructive for exploring four of the most frequently offered explanations for the link between crime rates and changes in the system and the legislative environment (i.e., administrative discretion, compositional shifts in the release cohorts, deterrence and incapacitation, and strained resources). In this we were not disappointed. Close examination of survival curves and hazard rates over the three-year follow-up period as well as those parolees released under the provisions of the PMA yielded much food for thought. Administrative practices (e.g., changes in technical revocations) accounted for some of the variation, but not all. Cohort composition also accounted for some of the variation (the 1986 cohort consisted of proportionally more high-risk parolees as did the PMA cohort).

The first piece of evidence indicating a potential reduced deterrent effect came in the form of increased repetitious offending patterns. Judging from a cross-tabulation of prior incarceration offense by return offense for those who were returned within thirty-six months, the pattern is clear. Parolees with a prior property offense, if returned to prison, were increasingly likely to have been returned for a subsequent property offense (52 percent for the 1984 cohort, 60 percent for the 1985 cohort, 59 percent for the 1986 cohort and 70 percent for the 1987 cohort).

The most dramatic increase in repetitious offending, which occurred among those released in 1987, corresponded to the period when publicity surrounding the crowded prison system and its revolving doors peaked. In addition, signs of shifting sentencing policies were quite evident by 1987. There was a substantial decline in the proportion of sentence served (at a time when the average sentence length was increasing), a considerable increase in the number of persons paroled from prison, and a dramatic increase in the proportion of persons paroled at their initial parole hearing (from approximately 40 percent in the early 1980s to approximately 80 percent by 1989).

While a good deal of the differential failure rates for the PMA releasees can be attributed to compositional differences, there is also some indirect evidence that the accelerated release may have further reduced the deterrent effect of prison. This is evidenced by the substantially higher repetitious offending of PMA releasees compared even to the baseline 1987 cohort. Seventy percent of parolees in the baseline cohort, who had served a sentence for property offenses and who were returned to prison, were returned for another property offense. The comparable figure for the PMA cohort was 85 percent.

Our comparison of national, Texas, and California data in chapter 7 was an attempt to explore this issue of a reduced deterrent effect further. While California expanded its prison capacity and implemented determinate sentencing, property crime rates declined and then essentially stabilized. Does this indicate that California's massive prison expansion was deterring property offenders? The answer is unclear, especially since the national property crime rates followed essentially the same pattern and most states did not expand their prison capacity at anywhere near the scale found in California. What is suggested is that a combination of factors may have eroded the deterrent effect of prison among property offenders.

The increase in return-to-prison rates in Texas as well as repetitious offending may have been the result in part of a decreased deterrent effect stemming from a prison system filled to capacity; an accompanying increased tendency among Parole Board members to release persons after their initial hearing; legislation providing for the additional early release of property offenders (the PMA); and finally, legislation that awarded good-time credits from a prior incarceration to parolees who were returned to prison for a technical revocation (S.B. 1167). It is also possible that varying economic conditions in Texas and California may have contributed in important ways to the noted patterns among property offenders.

This same comparative analysis of national, Texas, and California data suggests substantially different conclusions when it comes to violent crime patterns. There was not the same increase in repetitious offending patterns among these individuals. Nor was there any detectable difference in the statewide violent crime rate trends. In this sense, the quadrupling of prison capacity in California appeared to have little payoff when compared to Texas where, instead of a massive building program, caps were placed on admissions and an equally impressive expansion of parole was implemented. However, just as varying economic conditions introduce a note of caution when drawing conclusions for property offenders, it is important to note that the major group excluded from the most liberal provisions of early release were those serving time for violent crime. In this sense it is possible that a selective effect of criminal sanctions became operable.

The Front Door Solution: Intermediate Sanctions

One popular alternative solution to crowded prisons is the development of sanctions designed to divert convicted offenders from prison. These alternative sentences include probation, intensive supervision probation, boot camps, restitution centers, residential treatment centers, specialized case loads, and electronic monitoring. The popularity of probation-type sentences is evidenced by the rise in the probation population during the 1980s. Nationwide in 1980, there were some 1,100,000 adults under supervision in state probation departments. By 1989, this had increased to numbers approaching 2,500,000, representing an approximate 130 percent increase in just nine years, an increase that far outstripped increases in the resident population of the nation. In 1980, there were 645 probationers per 100,000 adult resident population. By the year's end in 1989, there were 1,369 probationers per 100,000 population, representing a 112 percent increase between 1980 and 1989. The increase in the probation population also far outpaced the increase in the crime rate, indicating a significantly higher likelihood of a sentence of probation by the end of the decade. Texas has relied heavily on probation as an alternative to incarceration. The probation rate in Texas in 1989 was the second highest in the nation, with 2,419 probationers per 100,000 population.

While our analysis does not focus on the success of intermediate sanctions, it is important to briefly address what we do know from other sources. Clearly, sentences like probation may have a short term impact on the prison population. If an offender who otherwise would have been sent to prison is diverted through probation, then one less inmate is incarcerated. Thus, if the goal is to reduce the prison population through diversion, probation works in the short term. The obvious question is, however, What are the longer term consequences? Petersilia and Turner

(1986, v) conducted an analysis of the success of probationers in California and concluded:

> These findings led us to believe that the majority of felons who are placed on probation in California constitute a serious threat to the public and that the increasing use of probation as a sentence for felons is a high-risk gamble. Our findings also showed that with the information currently available to (or legally usable by) the courts, it was not possible to improve the prediction of recidivism to more than 20 percent above chance.

Similar conclusions emerged from an analysis of probation in Texas (Arrigona and Fabelo 1988). This research indicated that while a relatively small percentage of probationers actually are revoked to prison (9.5 percent in 1987), probation revocations constituted over one-third of all TDC admissions in that year. Thus, it appears that in Texas, probation revocations significantly contributed to the prison population, reinforcing the idea that while probation may be a short-term solution to prison crowding, in the longer term, this intermediate sanction is less promising.

Mullen (1987, 91) suggests that one primary reason probation may not be a successful long-term strategy has to do with the allocation of resources in the criminal justice system.

> Consider the dilemma of probation—now the most widely used nonprison sanction. Probation capacity is not defined by bricks and mortar; nor have overloaded probation caseloads been the subject of judicial challenge. But the same loss of correctional control has resulted from the failure to establish sentencing standards that recognize capacity limitations. While prison crowding dominates the news, there are about three times as many offenders being supervised in the community. Since probation has become a vast dumping ground for all kinds of petty criminals and lesser felons—and the caseload of a single probation officer may number in the hundreds—it is hardly surprising that judges worry about the quality of supervision and researchers confirm their worst fears by suggesting that placing felons on probation constitutes a serious threat to public safety. . . . The new intermediate sanctions are unlikely to solve this dilemma unless capacity limitations are carefully installed and rigorously enforced.

What about the argument that probation and other prison alternatives are significantly cheaper than prison? Petersilia and Turner addressed this assumption in their analysis of probation in California. Their findings challenge the common wisdom on the relative cost of probation by taking into account not only the cost of supervision but also the costs associated with recidivism. While prison is clearly more expensive than probation, Petersilia and Turner suggest that probation involves considerably higher secondary costs than is commonly assumed.

It is also the case that the phenomenon commonly referred to as *net widening* has reduced the cost effectiveness of the expanded use of alternatives to prison. It takes but little thought to realize that if the expanded use of alternatives is driven not by those who would otherwise end up in prison, but by those who would have been released or sentenced to even less-restrictive sanctions, reductions in cost will be minimal and perhaps even escalate over a sanctioning scheme void of alternatives to prison. While the population as a whole is aging, historically signaling a drop in the crime rate, other factors, such as the growth in the minority population, gang activity and the powerful impact of street drugs, have nullified and likely will continue to nullify the imact of an aging population. In response, many jurisdictions in Texas and other states are increasingly devoting substantial amounts of resources to specialized probation caseloads. These programs for the mentally retarded, juveniles, sex offenders, alcohol and drug dependancy, child abuse, battering intervention, vocation training and education, among others are designed for diversion from prison. Since they are less costly than prison, these programs will save state and local dollars—*if they successfully divert offenders*. The problem is that we have precious little information regarding the short and long term success of such programs. We wish to stress the need to systematically evaluate the longer term success or failure of such programs and thus provide the means to make well informed policy decisions and implement programs that impact the crime rate and help alleviate prison crowding, not exascerbate it.

Increasing Prison Capacity

An internal Department of Justice memo exemplifies the popular political perspective of increasing prison capacity in order to reduce the crime rate:

> The inmate population is growing at an average rate of 15 percent a year. The Department estimates that given current capacity and only with the additions envisioned by the administration's current plan, overcrowding will increase to at least 72 percent by 1997. The demand for prison space thus will rise, but so will the voices of those who say we need fewer prisons and more "alternatives" to incarceration. We must take the side of more prisons, and to polarize the issue we must attack those by name (such as Senator Paul Simon) who take the other approach. We must stress why prisons are necessary by discussing retribution, deterrence, and incapacitation. Overall, of course, we must make the case that public safety demands more prisons. (Office of the Attorney General, Memorandum for Heads of Department Components, February 22, 1988 cited in Marcus 1988)

While several states have increased their prison capacity, it is argued that the costs of constructing prisons as well as the costs of maintaining inmates makes this a difficult if not totally unrealistic solution. It is estimated that there are, as this is being written, 67,000 new prison beds under construction in the United States and 90,000 more are planned. Those that are currently under construction will cost an estimated $3 billion (Durham 1991, 31). Over and above cost, Gottfredson (1987, 149) has questioned the wisdom of increasing prison capacity without carefully estimating future demand.

> Many prisons have been built on the argument of expected need. But that argument must be faulted on two main grounds. First, it requires the questionable assumption either that the present use of institutions is desirable or that use will nevertheless continue much as in the past . . . Minimally, projections of prison space needs ordinarily require the assumption that policy will not change or will change only slowly . . . Second, even if these more fundamental challenges should fail, the argument falters on our presently weak abilities to forecast crime and imprisonment.

There is another reason why, in many instances, prison construction may not be the panacea it appears to be. It is fairly clear today that in states where prison crowding is a problem, judges and prosecutors have adjusted their sentencing recommendations and policies toward sentences designed to divert offenders from prison. It has been argued that prison populations are capacity driven; thus, when capacity is increased, all else being equal, cells are quickly filled with eligible offenders.

California provides a good example of how prison construction may not necessarily reduce crowding. As we have noted, California undertook a massive prison construction program during the 1980s, resulting in a fourfold increase in the inmate population. Today, there are 101,000 prisoners in the California Department of Corrections. As of 1987, the California prison system was operating at 170 percent of its self-defined capacity. What has produced this crowding problem in California? Austin (1989, 3) provides one important piece of the puzzle.

> In 1987, there were 62,729 admissions received by the CDC, of which 31,581 (or 50.3 percent) were parole violators. In other words, California's criminal justice system has been spending more resources on recycling prisoners released to parole than on new offenders being sentenced directly by the courts.

More recently, the Center on Juvenile and Criminal Justice reported that in 1989, nearly 40,000 parole violators were returned to the California Department of Corrections. A summary of the center's report, presented in the Criminal Justice Newsletter (1991, 2), notes "most California parolees will leave prison with no marketable skills or job experience, no high school diploma, a 6th grade reading level, and a drug problem. In 1988, only 4 percent of the male prison parole population participated in prerelease programming, a situation that has not changed markedly. Fewer that 3 percent received drug treatment."

Replicating California's building frenzy, in 1991 Texas voters passed a $1.1 billion bond package for the construction of 25,000 new prison cells. A report recently published by the Texas Comptroller of Public Accounts (1992) notes that when current correction construction is completed in 1996, the Texas prison capacity will consist of nearly 81,200 prison beds and an additional 12,000 substance abuse treatment beds. This construction will represent a 250 percent increase since 1980. The report concludes (93):

> As high as these figures are, Texas will almost certainly need more prisons. The Texas Criminal Justic Policy Counsil estimates that by 1998, the state will need an additional 28,552 beds, over and above currently scheduled expansions to deal with the jail backlog problem. These additional prison beds will cost the state approximately $859 million to construct and an addition $296 million to operate.

What can the state expect with regard to public safety and the crime rate after this expansion of prison capacity. Our comparison of Texas and California indicates that the impact of prison construction on the crime rate is minimal at most. Moreover, the observation that over 50 percent of new admissions to California prisons are parole violators indicates that Texas can expect to see its prison's revolving doors turn at an even more rapid rate than they have in the past.

Reflecting an awareness of these bleak predictions of a minor return from a very large investment of the taxpayers' money, the 72nd session of the Texas Legislature in 1991 established the Texas Punishment Standards Commission to study the issue yet one more time and make recommendations. In particular the Commission was asked to propose legislation to (1) revise punishments for criminal offenses, (2) expand the capacity of state prisons and local jails and community corrections facilities, (3) revise probation and parole laws, and (4) expand probation and parole systems, including special supervision and treatment programs.

During the next year the Commission established a research team and held approximately 50 public meetings across the state to receive testimony from over 500 people. The findings had a familiar ring.

The criminal justice system in Texas, the Commission concluded, was in dire need of reform:

- Despite the costly prison expansion over the last decade, the Texas violent crime rate continues to rise and prisons remain filled beyond capacity.
- The increased rate of incarceration has crowded the prison system to the point that the sanction seems meaningless to both the public and practitioners; felons serve 13 percent of their sentence, or an average of 11.2 months in prison; and
- Payments to counties as reimbursement for housing the overflow of state inmates, plus fines, could approach $1 billion in the next biennium. (Texas Punishment Standards Commission 1992, i)

Given these conclusions, the Commission felt that simply expanding prison and parole capacity would not be enough. The legislature would have to come up with something better.

This something included sentencing law changes as well as recommendations regarding the expansion of prison facilities and alternatives to incarceration, but perhaps most dramatic in terms of the present study was the recommendation that the system of parole as a form of early release for offenders should be abolished.

This recommendation was driven in large measure by the Commission's desire to reform existing laws to better reflect "truth in sentencing." It was hypocritical in the extreme, Commission members felt, to sentence convicted felons to long prison terms and then to see these persons serve only 15 to 20 percent of the original time, in large measure because of crowded prison conditions.

To reduce this hypocrisy and enhance "truth in sentencing," the Commission proposed that the state's Penal Code be revised so that offenders would serve at least 80 percent of their time. Without further changes this would quickly bankrupt the state. Money would continue to be poured down the black hole of prison construction. Hence the Commission also proposed a new sentencing scheme wherein offenses would be ranked from capital murder, with sentences of death, life without parole, or life with parole, to 4th degree felonies where the potential sentences would be 1 to 4 years of mandatory community supervision which could include up to six months in jail and up to two years in a community corrections facility. In each of the new felony categories, sentences could be enhanced depending on the offender's prior criminal history.

Unfortunately, the Commission's own projections indicated that the shorter sentence and longer proportion of sentence served scheme would not do much to reduce the existing demand for expanded prison capacity. While prisoners would be shifted around to different types of facilities the Commission concluded that by 1998 "more offenders will be incarcerated under the proposal than under the status quo (133,310 versus 123,506)" (Texas Punishment Standards Commission 1992, Report 6). Nor did the Commission see any indication that ever increased incarceration rates would do much to reduce the public's primary concern, the rate of violent crime.

Going beyond their original mandate, the Commission noted that the answer was not to be found in more cellblocks but in programs to strengthen early childhood development and child-parent programs. In this sense, the Commission's conclusion reiterated what virtually every sentencing commission set up over the past three decades has found. It is a conclusion with which we heartily concur.

At the end of this work, it bears repeating that we are expecting far too much from our correctional institutions. Crime is so deeply embedded in the social fabric—in early childhood development, in the debilitating effects of drug abuse, and in disrupted networks of support in decaying urban neighborhoods and public school systems that expanding prison capacity to get offending persons off the street is likely to have at best only marginal effects on the crime rate. Criminals out of action and away at prison are easily replaced by new offenders. Until we begin to reduce the criminal replacement factor, we are going to be chasing an elusive goal, engaged in rhetoric-rich and proposal-poor debates over tough-minded crime policies.

Appendix A
Salient Factor Score

	DPO/PCW NO. ________	
Name: ________________	TDC NO. ____________	
Other State Name: ________	OTHER PRISON NO. ____	

A. Prior Convictions (Adult or Juvenile)	0 Prior = 3 1 Prior = 2 2 Prior = 1 3 or more = 0	________
B. Prior Incarcerations (Adult or Juvenile)	0 Prior = 3 1 Prior = 2 2 Prior = 1 3 or more = 0	________
C. Age at First Incarceration	26 yrs or older = 2 25 − 18 = 1 17 or younger = 0	________
D. Commitment Offense	Did not involve auto theft, burglary, or forgery = 1 Involved auto theft, burglary, or forgery = 0	________
E. Parole or Probation Revoked	Never = 2 Once = 1 More than once = 0	________
F. Drug and/or Alcohol Dependence	No history = 1 Otherwise = 0	________
G. Employment	6 months last 2 years = 1 Otherwise = 0	________
H. Education	Completed 12th Grade (GED) = 1 Otherwise = 0	________

I. Release Plan	Includes employment = 1 Otherwise = 0	____________
	TOTAL	____________

Score	*Risk*
0–4	HIGH
5–10	MEDIUM
11–15	LOW

UNIT SUPERVISOR INITIAL _____ DATE _____

Appendix B
Texas Board of Pardons and Paroles (BPP) Regions

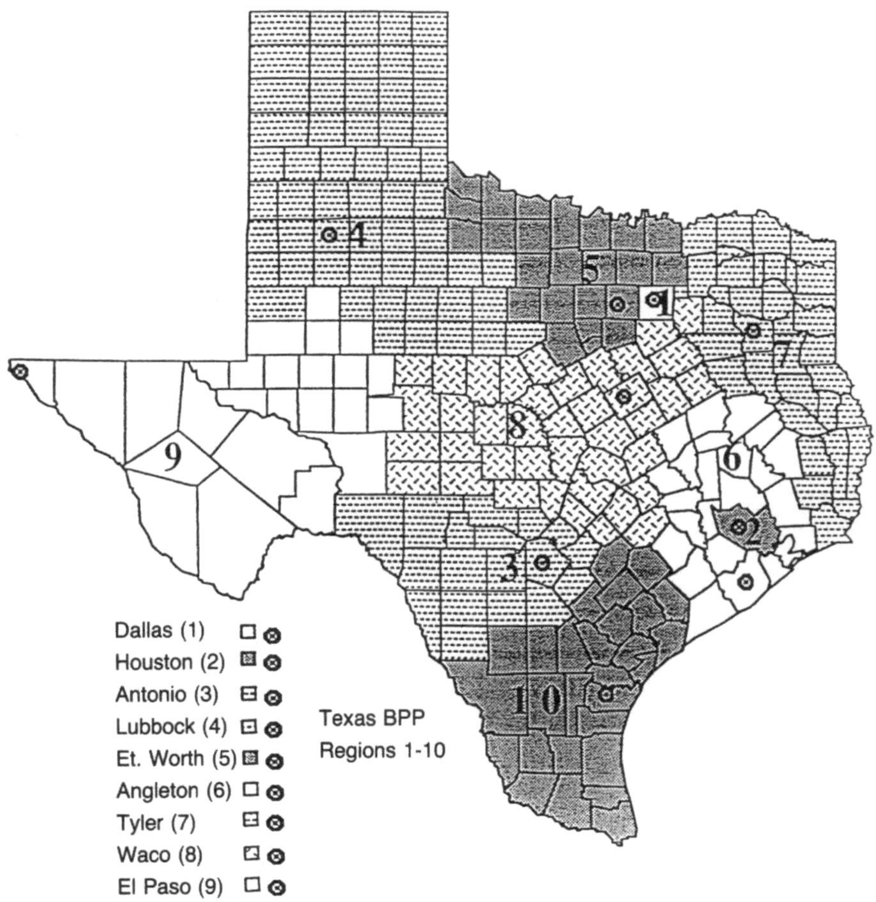

Map courtesy of Greg Markley, Director, Staff Development Division

References

Allison, P., 1984. *Event History Analysis: Regression for Longitudinal Event Data*. Sage University Paper Series on Quantitative Applications in the Social Sciences, no. 07–046. Beverly Hills: Sage Publications.

American Civil Liberties Union, 1988. *National Prison Project: Status Report the Courts and Prisons*. Washington: American Civil Liberties Union.

Arrigona, N., and T. Fabelo., 1988. Probation and prison populations. Austin: Criminal Justice Policy Council.

Austin, J., 1986. Using early release to relieve prison crowding. *Crime and Delinquency* 32:391–403.

Austin, J., 1987. "Success and failure on parole in California: A preliminary evaluation." National Council on Crime and Delinquency.

Austin, J., 1989. The consequences of determinate sentencing, punishment, and incapacitation on parole performance. San Francisco: National Council on Crime and Delinquency.

Banks, J., A.L. Porter, R.L. Rardin, T.R. Silver, and V.E. Unger., 1977. *Summary phase I evaluation of intensive special probation project*. Washington. National Institute of Law Enforcement and Criminal Justice.

Beck, E.M. and S.E. Tolnay., 1990. The killing fields of the deep south. *American Sociological Review* 55: 526–39.

Between Prison and Probation—Intermediate Punishments in a Rational Sentencing System., 1990. National Institute of Justice Reports. January/ February 9.

Blackmore, J. and J. Welsh., 1983. Selective incapacitation. *Crime and Delinquency*. 29:504–28.

Blumstein, A., 1983. Prisons: Population, capacity and alternatives. In *Crime and Public Policy*, edited by J.Q. Wilson. San Francisco: ICS Press.

Blumstein, A., J. Cohen, S. Martin, and M. Tonry, eds., 1983. *Research on sentencing: The search for reform*. 2 Vols. Washington. National Academy Press.

Blumstein, A., J. Cohen, and D. Nagin, eds., 1978. *Deterrence and incapacitation: Estimating the effects of criminal sanctions on crime rates*. Washington. National Academy of Sciences.

Brown, B.W., H. Walker, M. Schimek, and P.T. Wright., 1979. A life table package for SPSS. *American Sociological Review* 33:225–27.

Byrne, J., A. Lurigio, and C. Baird. "The effectiveness of the new intensive supervision programs." *Research in Corrections*, edited by J. Petersilia and S. Turner. Santa Monica: Rand Corporation.

Bureau of Justice Statistics, U.S. Department of Justice., 1978. Census of local jails—1978. Washington.

—— 1984, Returning to prison. Washington.

—— 1987, Prisoners in 1986.

—— 1989, Recidivism of prisoners released in 1983. Washington.

—— 1989a, Census of local jails—1988. Washington.

—— 1989b, Recidivism of prisoners released in 1983. Washington.

—— 1990, Probation and parole 1989. Washington.

—— 1991a, Prisoners in 1990.

—— 1991b, *Sourcebook of criminal justice statistics—1990*. Washington.

California Blue Ribbon Commission on Inmate Population Management. 1990. *Final Report*, January 3.

California Department of Corrections. 1984. Population projections, Fiscal Years 1984–85 through 1988–89, Offender information services branch. Sacramento. California Department of Correction.

Cantor, D. and K.C. Land., 1985. Unemployment and crime rates in the post–World War II United States. *American Sociological Review* 50:317–32.

Carr-Hill, G. and R. Carr-Hill., 1972. Reconviction as a process. *British Journal of Criminology* 12:35–43.

Chaiken, M.R. and J.M. Chaiken., 1984. Offender types and public policy. *Crime and Delinquency*. 30:195–226.

Chiricos, T.G., 1987. Rates of crime and unemployment. *Social Problems* 34:187–212.

Clarke, S.H., 1974. Getting 'em out of circulation. *Journal of Criminal Law and Criminology*. 65:528–35.

Cohen, J., 1983. "Incapacitation as a strategy for crime control: Possibilities and pitfalls." In *Crime and justice*, edited by M. Tonry and N. Morris. Chicago: University of Chicago Press.

Cohen, J., 1978. "The incapacitative effect of imprisonment: A critical review of the literature." In *Deterrence and incapacitation*, edited by A. Blumstein et al. Washington. National Academy of Sciences.

Cohen, L. and K.C. Land., 1987. Age structure and crime. *American Sociological Review*. 52:170–83.

Conrad, J.P., 1985. *The dangerous and the endangered*. Lexington, MA: Heath.

Cook, P.J. and G.A. Zarkin., 1985. Crime and the business cycle. *Journal of Legal Studies*. XIV:115–29.

Criminal Justice Newsletter., 1991. Probation and parole. 22:1–2.

Devine, J.A., J.F. Sheley, and M.D. Smith., 1988. Macroeconomic and social-control policy influences on crime rate changes, 1948–1985. *American Sociological Review* 53:407–14.

Durham, A., 1991. Then and now: The fruits of late 20th century penal reform. *Federal Probation*. September:28–35.

Ekland-Olson, S., 1986. "Crowding, Social Control and Prison Violence: Evidence from the Post-*Ruiz* Years in Texas," *Law and Society Review* 20:389–421.

Ekland-Olson, S., J. Lieb, and L. Zurcher., 1984. The paradoxical impact of criminal sanctions. *Law and Society Review* 18:159–78.

Ekland-Olson, S. and W. Kelly., 1989. Justice under pressure. Paper presented at symposium, American Society of Criminology meetings, Reno, Nevada, November 9–10.

Ekland-Olson, S., M. Supancic, J. Campbell, and K. Lenihan., 1983. Post release depression and the importance of familial support. *Criminology* 21:253–75.

Ekland-Olson, S., W.R. Kelly, and M. Eisenberg., 1992. "Crime and Incarceration: Some Comparative Findings From the 1980s," *Crime and Delinquency* 38:392–416.

Feeley, M., 1989. The significance of prison conditions cases. *Law and Society Review* 23:273–82.

Feeley, M. and R.A. Hanson., 1990. "The impact of judicial intervention on prisons and jails: A framework for analysis and a review of the literature." In *Courts, corrections and the constitution*, edited by J. DiIulio. New York: Oxford University Press.

Feinberg, S.E., 1977. *The analysis of cross-classified data*. Cambridge: MIT Press.

Gaes, G., 1985. "The Effects of Overcrowding in Prison." In *Crime and Justice: Annual Review of Research*, edited by M. Tonry and N. Morris. Chicago: University of Chicago Press.

Gibbs, J.P., 1975. *Crime, punishment, and deterrence*. New York: Elsevier.

Goodman, L.A., 1972a. A modified multiple regression to the analysis of dichotomous variables. *American Sociological Review* 37:28–46.

—— 1972b, A general model for the analysis of surveys. *American Journal of Sociology* 77:1035–86.

Gottfredson, D., 1987. "The problem of prison crowding: A system out of control." In *America's correctional crisis: Prison populations and public policy*, edited by S. Gottfredson and S. McConville. New York: Greenwood Press.

Gottfredson, D. and M. Tonry., 1987. *Crime and justice: An annual review of research*. Chicago: The University of Chicago Press.

Gottfredson, M.R. and T. Hirschi., 1990. *A general theory of crime*. Stanford: Stanford University Press.

Greenberg, D.F., 1975. The incapacitation effect of imprisonment. *Law and Society Review* 9:541–80.

Greenwood, P., 1983. *Selective Incapacitation*. Santa Monica: Rand Corporation.

Greenwood, P. and A. Abrahamse., 1982. "Controlling the crime rate through imprisonment." In *Crime and Public Policy*, edited by J.Q. Wilson. San Francisco: Institute for Contemporary Studies.

Greenwood, P. and S. Turner., 1987. Selective incapacitation revisited. Santa Monica: Rand Corporation.

Harris, M.K. and D.P. Spiller., 1977. *After Decision*: Implementation of Judicial Decrees in Correctional Settings. Washington D.C.: American Bar Association.

Hanushek, E. and J. Jackson., 1977. *Statistical methods for social scientists*. New York: Academic Press.

Hirsch, A. von., 1985. *Past or future crimes?* New Brunswick, NJ: Rutgers University Press.

Hirsch, A. von and D. Gottfredson., 1983–84. Selective incapacitation. *Review of Law and Social Change*. 12: 11–51.

Hirschi, T. and M. Gottfredson., 1983. Age and the explanation of crime. *American Journal of Sociology* 89: 552.

Hoffman, P. and B. Stone-Meierhoefer., 1979. Post release arrest experiences of federal prisoners. *Journal of Criminal Justice* 7:193–216.

Irwin, J., 1970. *The felon*. Englewood Cliffs, NJ: Prentice-Hall.

Issac, L. and L. Griffin., 1989. Ahistoricism in time-series analyses of historical process. *American Sociological Review* 54:873–90.

Jacobs, J., 1980. "The prisoners' rights movement and its impact 1960–1980." *In Crime and Justice: An Annual Review of Research*, edited by N. Morris and M. Tonry Chicago: The University of Chicago Press: 429.

Kelly, W.R. and S. Ekland-Olson., 1991. The response of the criminal justice system to prison overcrowding. *Law and Society Review* 25:601–20., 1992. Prison crowding and parole survival. *Law and Society Review*.

Klein, S. and M. Caggiano., 1986. The prevalence, predictability and policy implications of recidivism. Santa Monica: Rand Corporation.

Klockars, C.B., 1974. *The professional fence*. New York: Free Press.

Kmenta, J., 1971. *Elements of econometrics* New York: Macmillan.

Knoke, D. and P. Burke., 1980. *Log-linear models*. Sage University Paper Series on Quantitative Applications in the Social Sciences, no.07–020. Beverly Hills: Sage Publications.

Langan, P.A., 1991. America's soaring prison population. *Science* 251:1568–73.

McCord, W. and J. McCord., 1959. *Origins of crime: A new evaluation of the Cambridge-Somerville study*. New York: Columbia University Press.

Mackenzie, D.L. and B.G. Parent., 1991. "Shock incarceration and prison crowding in Louisiana." *Journal of Criminal Justice* 19:225–37

Maltz, M. and R. McCleary., 1977. The mathematics of behavioral change. *Evaluation Quarterly* 1:421–438.

Marcus, R., 1988. "Justice department memo: Polarizes debate." Washington Post. Feb. 26 P. A4.

Marquart, J.W., S. Ekland-Olson, and J.R. Sorensen., 1989. Gazing into the crystal ball: Can jurors accurately predict dangerousness in capital cases?" *Law and Society Review* 23:101–20.

Martin, S.J. and S. Ekland-Olson., 1987. *Texas prisons*. Austin: Texas Monthly Press.

Methuin, E.H., 1991. "Let's lock up more criminals—it works." *The Houston Chronicle* November 10. Dutlook.

Minor, W.W. and M. Courlander., 1979. The post-release trauma thesis: A reconsideration of the rise of early parole failure. *Journal of Research in Crime and Delinquency* 16:273–93.

Monahan, J., 1981. *Predicting violent behavior: An assessment of clinical techniques*. Beverly Hills. Sage. Publications.

Morris, N. and M. Tonry., 1990. Between prison and probation—Intermediate punishments in a rational sentencing system. *National Institute of Justice Reports*. U.S. Department of Justice. Washington.

Morris, N. and M. Miller., 1985. Predictions of dangerousness. *Crime and Justice: An Annual Review of Research*. Chicago: University of Chicago Press.

Mullen, J., 1987. "State responses to prison crowding: The politics of change. In *America's correctional crisis: Prison populations and public policy*, edited by S. Gottfredson and S. McConville. New York: Greenwood Press.

Parker, R. and A. Horwitz., 1986. Unemployment, crime and imprisonment. *Criminology* 24:751–73.

Patterson, O., 1982. *Slavery and social death: A comparative study*. Cambridge: Harvard University Press.

Petersilia, J., S. Turner, and J. Peterson., 1986. "Prison versus probation in california: Implications for crime and offender recidivism." Santa Monica: Rand Corporation.

Rosenfeld, R. and K. Kempf., 1991. The scope and purposes of corrections. *Crime and Delinquency* 37: 481–505.

Rossi, P. H., R. Berk, and K. Lenihan., 1980. *Money, work, and crime: Experimental evidence*. New York: Academic Press.

Schmidt, P. and A. Witte., 1988. *Predicting recidivism using survival models*. New York: Springer-Verlag.

Sherman, L. and R. Berk., 1984. The specific deterrent effects of arrest for domestic assualt. *American Sociological Review* 49:261–71.

Sherman, M. and G. Hawkins., 1981. *Imprisonment in America: Choosing the future*. Chicago: The University of Chicago Press.

Sorenson, A., 1977. "Estimating rates from retrospective questions." In *Sociological Methodology 1977*, edited by D. Heise. San Francisco: Jossey-Bass.

Steffenmeier, D. and M. Harer., 1991. Did crime rise or fall during the Reagan presidency? *Journal of Research in Crime and Delinquency*. 28:330–59.

Stollmack, S. and C. Harris., 1974. Failure rate analysis applied to recidivism data. *Operations Research* 23:1192–1205.

Taggart, W.A., 1989. Redefining the power of the federal judiciary. *Law and Society Review* 23:241–71.

Texas Board of Pardons and Paroles, 1970–90. "Annual Statistical Report."

Texas Comptroller of Public Accounts. *Texas Crime, Texas Justice: A Report From the Texas Performance Review*. Austin, Texas: Office of the Comptroller.

Texas Department of Corrections, 1972–90. "Fiscal Year Statistical Report."

Texas Punishment Standards Commission, 1992. "Draft Recommendation, for Commission Review." Austin, Texas.

Thornberry, T. and J. Jacoby., 1979. *The criminally insane: A community follow-up of mentally ill offenders*. Chicago: University of Chicago Press.

Tonry, M., 1987. "Prediction and classification: Legal and ethical issues." In *Crime and Justice: An Annual Review of Research*. Chicago: The University of Chicago Press.

Tuma, N. and M. Hannan., 1978. "Approaches to the censoring problem in analysis of event histories." In *Sociological Methodology 1979*, edited by K. Schuessler. San Francisco: Jossey-Bass.

Van Dine, S., J.P. Conrad, and S. Dinitz., 1979. *Restraining the wicked: The incapacitation of the dangerous criminal*. Lexington, MA: Heath.

Wilson, J.Q., 1975. *Thinking about crime*. New York: Basic Books.

Wilson, J.Q. and P. Cook., 1985. Unemployment and crime—What is the connection? *The Public Interest* 79:3–8.

Wilson, W.J., 1987. *The truly disadvantaged: The inner city, the underclass, and public policy*. Chicago: University of Chicago Press.

Wolfgang, M., R. Figlio, and T. Sellin., 1972. *Delinquency in a birth cohort*. Chicago: University of Chicago Press.

Zedlewski, E.W., 1987. Making confinement decisions. Washington: National Institute of Justice.

Zimring, F.E., 1990. Correctional growth in context. Paper presented at conference, Growth and Its Influence on Correctional Policy—Perspectives on the Report of the Blue Ribbon Commission. University of California, Berkeley, May 10–11.

Index

Research in Criminology

continued

Multiple Problem Youth:
Delinquency, Substance Use, and Mental Health Problems
D.S. Elliott, D. Huizinga and S. Menard

Selective Incapacitation and the Serious Offender:
A Longitudinal Study of Criminal Career Patterns
Rudy A. Haapanen

Deterrence and Juvenile Crime: Results from a National Policy Experiment
Anne L. Schneider

Understanding Crime Incidence Statistics:
Why the UCR Diverges from the NCS
Albert D. Biderman and James P. Lynch

Developments in Crime and Crime Control Research:
German Studies on Victims, Offenders, and the Public
Klaus Sessar and Hans-Jürgen Kerner (Eds.)

Human Development and Criminal Behavior:
News Ways of Advancing Knowledge
Michael Tonry, Lloyd E. Ohlin, and David P. Farrington, with
contributions by Kenneth Adams, Felton Earls, David C. Rowe,
Robert J. Sampson, and Richard E. Tremblay

MIX
Papier aus verantwortungsvollen Quellen
Paper from responsible sources
FSC® C105338

If you have any concerns about our products,
you can contact us on
ProductSafety@springernature.com

In case Publisher is established outside the EU,
the EU authorized representative is:
Springer Nature Customer Service Center GmbH
Europaplatz 3, 69115 Heidelberg, Germany

Printed by Libri Plureos GmbH
in Hamburg, Germany